The CEO Paradox

"Tom Horton has a good ear and piercing eye. His new book distills decades of being a leader and listening to and watching others into keen observations that will be useful to leaders everywhere."

Paul O'Neill, Chairman and CEO
Aluminum Company of America

"Tom Horton's new book is a perceptive look at the challenges facing today's CEOs. Its lessons of leadership should benefit managers at all levels."

J. W. Marriott, Jr.
Chairman of the Board and President
Marriott Corporation

"If you are a CEO, or want to be a CEO, or if you just work with CEOs, you should read Tom Horton's book. He knows as many CEOs as anyone in the world and his quotes and observations are authentic, instructive, and entertaining."

Robert W. Lear, Executive in Residence
Graduate School of Business, Columbia University
Former CEO
F. & M. Schaefer

"A fast and intriguing read. Horton catches the essence of the CEO's relationship with the various constituencies with which he or she has to deal on a regular basis. His book touches today's real issues of corporate governance and their implication for America's competitiveness."

Frederick W. Zuckerman
Senior Vice President and Treasurer
RJR Nabisco

"This book is not just for CEOs—but for all in positions of leadership. Anyone aspiring to advance should not just read this book—but study it page by page. They will learn more than from an entire year at most business schools."

Arthur C. Nielsen, Jr., Former Chairman and CEO
A. C. Nielsen Co.

"Horton tells it like it is, with a great blend of candor and humor. . . . You'll be a more effective CEO if you read it."

John H. Zimmerman, Senior Vice President
Corporate Human Resources
MCI Communications Corporation

"A wonderful book—a penetrating analysis of this important role in America's corporate hierarchy. It is full of wisdom and wit, and comes to the point quickly and easily on the many complex subjects covered."

Mathias J. DeVito, Chairman of the Board
President and CEO
The Rouse Company

"A masterful, and oftentimes emotional, review of the 'inside story' of what makes the CEO tick. . . . His conclusions are often alarmingly simple and to the point that CEOs are products of their own values and their ability to cope with conflict and opportunity at the same time."

Roy A. Herberger, Jr., President
American Graduate School of
International Management (Thunderbird)

"Tom Horton has captured the profile of CEOs in an easy to understand and stimulating style—a timely and actionable book for all managers. . . . I wish I'd had this book to read when I was striving to climb the corporate ladder. It would have eliminated many rungs."

Peter G. Scotese, Retired CEO
Springs Industries, Inc.

"The definitive book on leadership at the top. . . . Must reading for all those leaders close to or at the top of their enterprises."

H. L. Tower, Chairman of the Board
Stanhome Inc.

"*The CEO Paradox* is concise, to the point, and filled with valuable insights—a bit like having the mirror talk back! A great way to stimulate the mind of any manager on how to be more effective in the leadership role!"

Edward K. Trowbridge, Chairman and CEO
Atlantic Mutual Companies

"A practical, personal, and readable guide to the essential *meaning* of the job of the Chief Executive. In addition, *The CEO Paradox* is filled with remarkable insights about leadership and accountability that are useful to all managers at all organizational levels."

Richard G. Brandenburg, Dean and Professor
School of Business Administration
The University of Vermont

THE
CEO
PARADOX

*The Privilege
and Accountability
of Leadership*

Thomas R. Horton

American Management Association

New York • Atlanta • Boston • Chicago • Kansas City • San Francisco • Washington, D.C.
Brussels • Toronto • Mexico City

This book is available at a special
discount when ordered in bulk quantities.
For information, contact Special Sales Department,
AMACOM, a division of American Management Association,
135 West 50th Street, New York, NY 10020.

Library of Congress Cataloging-in-Publication Data

Horton, Thomas R.
    The CEO paradox : the privilege and accountability of leadership/
Thomas R. Horton.
      p.   cm.
    Includes bibliographical references and index.
    ISBN 0-8144-5093-8
    1. Chief executive officers.   2. Leadership.   3. Management.
I. Title.
HD38.2.H67   1992
658.4 —dc20   92-14650
                                                                 CIP

Printing number

10 9 8 7 6 5 4 3 2 1

To
Marilou
and to our three daughters,
Susan
Jean
Marilyn

Contents

Preface

In recent years, the chief executive has become a central character on the American stage, a cultural icon in our society, an object for serious scrutiny and trivial gossip. In short, a celebrity.

Books about, and by, CEOs have found their way to the best-seller lists. Celebrated for their achievements or vilified for their failures, those who hold the top positions of corporate command have become objects of public fascination, much like the explorers and inventors of earlier centuries. And this phenomenon is not limited to the United States. In Japan, such corporate chieftains as Akio Morita and the late Soichiro Honda command a level of respect once reserved for great samurai warriors. In visiting Prague less than a year after the "Velvet Revolution," I noted the autobiography of Thomas Bata, the Czech-born Canadian shoe manufacturer, centrally displayed in windows of virtually every bookstore. And in the former Soviet Union, thanks to *glasnost*, Lee Iacocca's writings are in as great a demand as George Orwell's.

At home, however, not all of these corporate celebrities are objects of admiration. Some are envied for their opulent life-styles and the prodigious rewards that make these possible. Indeed, the early 1990s have brought a tidal wave of anger at what many people regard as utter excess.

This preoccupation with chief executives extends beyond idle curiosity about the lives of the rich and famous to the question of what CEOs do and how they do it. There are other questions too: Are CEOs special people, unusual men and women destined from birth to be leaders? Or do they reach the top through some combination of talent and lucky circumstances? Do they owe their selection to some arbitrary god possessed of more humor than justice? And if some CEOs have "lucked out" over people more worthy than they, does their experience, once they reach the top, somehow transform them? For that matter, are CEOs really any different from ordinary mortals?

First of all, if my experience can serve as a guide, it can be said that they are certainly different from each other. And, to some degree, so are their jobs. There are differences between being a paid executive and working for a company you own. There are differences between the challenges of a $1 million operation and a $10 billion one. There are differences between publicly owned and privately held corporations. There are differences between not-for-profit and for-profit organizations. In the corporate world, there are differences between manufacturing firms and service companies. Within those two sectors, there are differences across industry lines, and even great variations among companies within the same industry.

However, the differences in working in such varied organizations as these tend to lessen the further up you go within them. After all, the job of the CEO is to lead, and this job requires that certain tasks be undertaken, tasks common to every kind of organization—planning, for example, and agenda setting. Certain skills of leadership must be mastered and deftly applied—delegation, team building, decision making, the management of corporate culture. The job of leader requires leadership behavior and a mastery of relationships with others, regardless of the setting. It requires, too, the ability to call on certain coping mechanisms as leaders attempt to manage activities foreign to them—or just to deal with the shortage of time and the complexities of fast-changing circumstances.

Moreover, successful leadership demands certain special qualities. Beyond intellectual capacity and interpersonal skills, it requires a desire to be held accountable. Yet there must be a willingness to let others run with the ball, and at times even call the plays. It requires the power to persuade and the open-mindedness to be persuaded, the readiness to take risks and to let others do so. Leadership demands tireless persistence. More than anything else, it calls for the ability to build enduring trust. The truth is that the tasks of a chief executive, and the qualities needed, are identical across all organizations, though in very different proportions at different times and in different cultures.

What *is* different are the CEOs themselves. These are men,

and increasingly women, who seem to have absolutely nothing in common with each other apart from their leadership roles. Their personalities, their beliefs, their backgrounds vary all over the map. Many have graduate degrees, some even Ph.D.s; some, even a few newly elected chieftains of large corporations, ended their formal education with high school. Each path to the top, from sales or finance or engineering or from the general counsel's post, represents a different story. CEOs go about their jobs in different ways, too. Some proceed with slow and analytical deliberation, while others count heavily on their instincts, firing first and aiming later.

Even within the same industry, and within the same specialized part of an industry, CEOs vary remarkably one from another. The particular approaches of one successful chief do not necessarily work well for another. Indeed, the best CEOs are unique, fully themselves, men and women who draw deeply on their inner resources and never stop learning and growing.

It is my conviction that the tasks of CEOs and the qualities needed by them for success are common to all true leaders at every level within an organization. The first-line manager, even one new to the job, must from time to time accomplish tasks not unlike those of the CEO, though at a very different level. And the qualities needed by a good first-line manager, one who is also a leader, are the same as those needed at the top. Of course, the CEO operates across a broader landscape, with a longer decision time span, and has far greater influence than others—but leadership, however you may choose to define it, is a constant.

Still, there is one indisputable difference between low- and middle-level leaders and CEOs: the CEO mystique. Books and articles written about chief executives tend to celebrate the magic of the job or the charisma of its incumbent. But those who have been CEOs, charismatic or not, know that there's precious little magic available to them—no sorcery, no tricks—just plain hard work.

Looked at objectively, the duties of the chief executive are large. But they are not mysterious, and they are certainly not beyond doing. One purpose of this book is to demystify the role of the chief executive—to make it understandable—and to suggest ways that the job can be done better. Along the way there are also suggestions about how managers at lower levels, at least those managers who act as leaders, can improve their performance as well.

CEOs bear an ultimate day-to-day responsibility to their customers and their employees that is different in degree from that of other managers. More significantly, they hold responsibility, as no others do or can, for the future. Decisions made at the top may have long-term consequences. And it is this aspect of the CEO's responsibility that distinguishes the position from the jobs of managers at lower levels—despite the many similarities that bind their tasks together.

What I've observed does not always square with what I've read about CEOs. I therefore believe that the celebrity aura (and the autobiographies that feed that aura, along with the endless writings about vision and the art of leadership) has somewhat obscured the public's understanding of what it is that CEOs do—and who they really are.

Effective leadership *is* an art. And, like other arts, it derives not just from genius but from a thorough mastery of the artist's craft. And that means practice. This, then, is a book about leadership and the special craft of the topmost job. Success in that job comes not from charisma but from mastery of essential skills and from practice.

Literally, chief executives learn their job on the job. It can't be learned in any other way. Entrepreneurs learn through trial and error as they build their companies. Corporate CEOs, including college presidents and others from the nonprofit sector, learn by observing what does and doesn't work on the way up. And for many, including myself, learning comes through observation of other successful chiefs. I've found the most interesting aspect of the top leader's job to be the limitless variety of ways in which success can be achieved.

To help accomplish the demystification of the CEO, I've tried to present a sampler of down-to-earth approaches taken by successful CEOs to the various tasks of leadership. In this selection of examples, I must admit to a certain bias, for I've chosen, not always consciously, to emphasize the leadership philosophies and practices that most closely conform to my own. This is a book neither of recipes for success nor of remedies for failure. It is simply an account of how I, and many others, have approached the challenge, and the profound privilege, of leadership.

Despite the great variety of approaches presented, however, they represent only a small sample. Great leaders lead in individualistic ways. By observing them, we can learn. I hope this book stimulates you to think about the practice and special craft of leadership and the way that craft can be developed.

Underlying the issue of leadership are serious questions regarding privilege—and accountability. The chief executive of any organization is the person ultimately accountable for its success or failure. But to just whom, other than the organization's owners, *is* the CEO accountable? To customers? To society? And just *how* is the chief held accountable, even to the owners? Who is being held accountable, and how, for the collapse of the savings and loan industry? For failed commercial banks? For underfunded pension plans? For inferior products, such as flawed medical devices? In what sense are today's leaders accountable?

And what about privilege? The person who accepts the risk that accompanies ultimate accountability surely deserves a just reward. But what *is* just? The average CEO of a large American corporation now draws down about $2 million annually. Some receive far more; a few, unprecedented amounts. Indeed, pay levels at the top have tripled over the past ten years, a period during which the take-home pay of many workers has failed to keep up with their needs—and a decade during which several American industries have been vanquished by their foreign competitors. Yet the proxy statement of the typical large American company provides descriptions (sometimes mysterious) of a bewildering array of kinds of executive compensation. Moreover, annual retirement pensions exceeding $1 million are no longer unusual. Beyond direct compensation and the opportunity to accumulate capital, there may be lavish executive perquisites—fleets of jet planes, for example. Some companies have even purchased residences for their chiefs. And should bail-out time arrive, there may be the prospect of a "golden parachute," a lump-sum payment equal to three or more times the CEO's annual salary and bonus, or some other severance arrangement designed to ensure a life of continued affluence.

In recent years, many observers, including some executive compensation specialists, have been asking, "How much is too much?" One highly regarded CEO observes that executive pay is often not linked to performance—and certainly not linked to how well the owners of the company do. He adds, "The only one who gets the short end of the stick is the shareholder." However, there are others who've been getting an even shorter end of that stick. In 1990 alone, nearly a million American managers earning more than $40,000 annually lost their jobs, as have millions of other employees during recent years. Is it fair during this era of downsizing for our corporate leaders to be rewarded at their current levels? And how much of their compensation is at risk? How much *should* be? Still, they hold the ultimate responsibility for their organizations' success or failure. And if a CEO has rescued a company, and in doing so has saved or created thousands of jobs, how much is enough?

In cases of blatant unfairness, who is responsible? The boards of directors, who establish compensation levels for their chief executives (and, not so incidentally, for themselves)? Just to whom are corporate directors accountable, and how privileged should *they* be?

Quite apart from fairness, does the sedan-chair-like treatment of many top executives distance them too far from the reality of their customers and employees? How well is American industry served by their current levels of compensation? And who is accountable for the demise of once profitable companies and whole industries?

The pages of this book contain no answers to these questions. Indeed, there are no general answers. The paradox of privilege and accountability can be resolved only by individual leaders of principle, men and women who are willing to confront it. Until those at the top perceive their accountability as a sacred trust, and accept only the privileges they fully deserve, the troubling CEO paradox will persist.

Acknowledgments

To several extraordinary leaders I have known, a great debt of gratitude is owed. The person most influential to my management philosophy has been Thomas J. Watson, Jr., now chairman emeritus of International Business Machines Corporation. A further debt is owed to many scholars, and a special one to Peter F. Drucker.

As to the book itself, it was Myles Thompson who first suggested I write a book for AMACOM, and the American Management Association's Arlene Bein who, after looking through some notes I'd made on the nature of the CEO's job, suggested I expand those notes into book form.

A number of people read parts of the manuscript and made suggestions: Frank Giglio, Marlene Groth, Susan Polos, Marilyn Thudium, and Peter Reid, who read it all and contributed most of the chapter and section titles. Fran Willis provided valuable information on corporate culture. Marilou Horton made important suggestions throughout its writing.

Patricia Haskell, agent and friend, helped to frame the premise of the book and provided valuable commentary on the manuscript. Carol Becker and Maureen Starkey processed all its many words, several times over, and Kate Pferdner managed the editing with care.

Finally, there is Adrienne Hickey, senior acquisitions editor at AMACOM, who shepherded the project from start to finish and whose insight is matched only by her tact—a rare person whose helpful criticisms come disguised as warm words of encouragement.

Chapter One

MEMORANDUM

TO: The Incoming Chief Executive Officer

FROM: The Outgoing Chief Executive Officer

Congratulations! Your election as my successor is a happy move both for the company and for you. Our directors could not have pleased me more. Surprisingly, I also find myself relieved, after these past ten years, to be turning over "the mantle of leadership." Until today, I had not recognized its full weight. And while it has been great fun (some of it more in retrospect than it was at the time), I realize I'm ready for a break. Knowing that you are up to the challenge—and raring to go—makes my exit much easier.

The many talks about leadership we've had over the past weeks should be ample evidence of my confidence in you. What I've tried to do is to pass along what I've picked up on the job and what I've learned by watching others.

Perhaps I was presumptuous in taking up so much of your time, but I needed to share my views and to solicit yours as well. Now I'm about to presume further! Attached is a long write-up based on the notes I used in those sessions. Think of it as part of my legacy. The rest of the legacy, of course, resides in the current shape of the company.

There are enormous problems to be solved. Some have just arrived on our doorstep, and some are old, intractable ones that have resisted my best efforts to resolve them. But there are also great opportunities, many of which I've failed to exploit. I am confident that you'll find ways to turn these

1

opportunities into profit and that your record will surpass mine. But as you will recall from our discussions, it won't really be "your" record, just as mine wasn't "mine." The first lesson of leadership is that it is not a one-person phenomenon: Results come from the combined efforts of every employee. But even with this combined effort, results cannot be achieved without leadership support, a concept that goes far beyond the old leader/follower theory.

Now for a few words about the write-up that follows. First, you don't have to read it—at least not now. Everything in it was covered in one way or another during our talks. And, of course, you won't have time to read it anyway, for the flood of paper that had been inundating my desk has just been diverted to yours. But I do hope that once in a while you will take the time to scan these pages and possibly to share some of them with others.

The reason for this is simple. When I first began putting these notes together, I tried to limit my efforts to topics that uniquely pertained to the job of CEO, but I quickly learned this wasn't possible. Some aspects of your job as CEO are unique, but there is much in common among all leadership jobs, whether it be that of first-line manager, senior staff head, or chief executive. After I had organized these notes into a readable form, I tried once more to put the CEO lore in one pile and the general leadership material in another—but again I found this to be impossible.

The truth is that management and leadership skills represent a continuum. There are times, for example, when first-line managers simply must take command, calling on their own instincts with little or no guidance from above. Similarly, there are times when chief executive officers, popularly thought to be autonomous, cannot act independently but instead must call on all their talents of persuasion to get their directors to go along in some new direction. Indeed, your people need the benefit of these thoughts more than you do.

In many ways your job and the jobs of your managers are alike. All of you depend on the results of others and the way they take responsibility. Over the years, I've noticed that responsibility usually falls to the person willing to take it, and your job will be much easier if you let others help carry the load. So if you find yourself in agreement with what I have written, please feel free to share these pages widely. More likely, you will want to put your own spin on my reflections, just as you will put your own mark on the company.

My mentoring is completed. I am about to go through what my friends say will be a difficult transition, though I don't yet see it that way. And you are about to go through an unusual transformation. Your life will change in profound and subtle ways, some unforeseeable to either of us.

Best wishes for the future. I won't be expecting too many calls from you, but you know how to reach me if you need to.

Good luck!

Chapter Two

You've Made It to the Top—Now What?

As a new CEO you may not feel different, but you are—especially in the eyes of others. You may be startled to notice how people you've known for a long time begin to look at you differently: Their eyes seem more sharply focused on you. Some people become conspicuously deferential. When you enter a room you've entered hundreds of times before, you suddenly command more attention. People listen more carefully, too. People you never saw taking notes before start taking notes. A special aura is beginning to embrace you, an aura of authority that comes with the job.

Donald Perkins, for ten years chief executive of Jewel Cos., describes this phenomenon. A friendly and outgoing leader, Perkins was troubled by what he calls the "silent pause that follows CEOs around an organization." Tom Watson, Jr., the legendary former chief executive of IBM, frequently expressed irritation over the deference shown him and avoided such executive trappings as limousines in an attempt to shatter the mystique. "I think a sense of humility is vital to running one of these jobs well," he said, "and the more humility the better."

In contrast, many CEOs revel in extensive trappings, setting themselves apart by perks unavailable to others and surrounding themselves with a coterie of executive assistants and other minions. In my view Watson handled this better than most, but however you handle it, you'll notice that the aura is always there. In some way, you have become an icon of sorts.

"I haven't changed," you may be saying to yourself, "but something's changed." A good rule to follow is this: Though you may seem different to others, try not to *be* different. Be yourself. But stay fully aware of the "silent pause" that comes with the CEO job and of its effects on other people. Just don't let it affect you.

This silent pause springs from the fact that you have a new-found significance to others. There is a change in what you mean to them, not just in degree but in kind. They feel that their future depends on you. To employees, you are no longer just another manager, though you may consider yourself such. Instead, you have become (for better or worse) a role model, playing a part you never auditioned for and perhaps did not want. You're now on center stage. Wherever you move, the spotlight follows you. As the drama unfolds, you may feel insecure. After all, there has been no rehearsal and there is no script. Still, you are expected to know your lines, for each word will be listened to and given significant weight.

A CEO hired from outside the company attracts even more scrutiny. "What do we have here?" people wonder. A savior, or a fearsome threat?

Your significance varies according to the circumstances of the audience. To employees, you are not just a role model but a guide to the future. "Where are we going and why?" they want to know. "How do we get there and when?" You are expected to have the answers. If the chief executive doesn't have these answers, then who does? Still, it is a wise CEO who knows that he or she does *not* have all the answers. At the beginning it takes a lot of digging even to find the right questions to ask.

Another role you play is that of inspiration giver. Everyone needs hope, especially in tough times, and you must be seen as

> You have become (for better or worse) a role model, playing a part you never auditioned for and perhaps did not want.

optimistic and a source of strength. (A CEO six months into his job recently asked me, "When do I start having fun?" My reply: "Probably not for a while, but you'd better start *looking* like you're having fun!") To many you are a father figure—with all the emotional baggage that implies. Admired or feared, loved or hated, you are seen as the ultimate holder of power, a person who can open the door of opportunity—or slam it shut. You hold enormous economic significance for your people, many of whom have second mortgages, college tuition loans, and other financial responsibilities. They long to see an upturn in the company's fortune as well as their own. You have become, too, a sort of mystery figure. Most people have no idea what you do or what the limits of your power and authority are. To some degree the CEO of even the most modern, high-tech company shares the aura of mystery and magic held by the aboriginal medicine man.

Bringing the Board on Board

How is it possible to play all of these roles? Or *is* it possible?

To members of the board of directors, you have a very different significance from the one you have for your employees. Formally and legally you report to the directors, who oversee your activities—and who ultimately pass judgment on your results. The board holds the power to remove you from office, yet its primary role is one of policy, not operations. Except in times of crisis, the influence of the directors on the company largely depends on how well you use their talents.

In many ways the directors are dependent on you. The way you lead the company can influence their reputations in the business community. You can bring them glory—or ignominy. How you are seen by your directors frequently depends on what you *let* them see. My advice: Let the board see a lot.

Board meetings are not just occasions for sharing good news or boring the directors with unexciting presentations. Though every board is different, my advice, while not original, is unbeatable: "No surprises." Remember, your performance can affect your directors' reputations. They need to know what is going on. Remember also: Directors are paid to represent the shareholders, whose long-term interests must be kept a high priority. The way you handle the circumstances of your business can make you either a hero or a bum in the eyes of your directors, and their assessment of your capability can change very quickly. Finally, if your board relationships are all sweetness and light, that's not great either. If there are no critics among your directors, you'd better recruit some. A board of close friends is no board at all.

Still, even if your directors do become your friends, or seem to, don't count on their friendship to see you through. Increasingly, boards are abandoning their custom of rubber-stamping their CEOs' plans. In 1992, for example, the General Motors Board of Directors demoted its president, and it replaced the chairman of its executive committee—a post until then held by GM's chairman and CEO—by an outside director.

Shareholders: Don't Keep Them in the Dark

Though you may have a say in who sits on the board of directors (and in most companies the board is still hand-picked by the CEO), your shareholders are another matter. They pick you—or at least your company. Because they are the company's owners, they, even more than the board, are the people (or institutions) to whom you ultimately report. And they have two very simple measures by which to judge your success: the size, and consistency, of dividends and the market value of their shares. Of course, many shareholders are interested in how you plan to achieve profitable growth, but most simply want persuasive evidence that you'll do so.

Because they own the company, shareholders deserve timely, forthright information. They need to know what happened yesterday that is affecting today's earnings. And they especially need to know what you're doing today to ensure future earnings. If you operate with your board in a no-surprise mode, as you should, then take this rule to the extreme with your shareholders: *"absolutely* no surprises!"

Going Public

If the board of directors and the shareholders think of you in one way, to others you have quite a different significance. To customers and the public at large you personify the organization. If you are not responsive, how can your people be expected to be responsive? As the CEO, you are expected to be able to cut through your company's bureaucracy like a laser beam, though at times your experience will suggest otherwise. Still, you wield the power; all the buttons are there for you to push.

In the communities in which your company operates, you are expected to support worthwhile organizations. Yet the shareholders want you to carefully husband their company's resources. Some will be less than thrilled to hear about the substantial contribution you just authorized in support of the local symphony orchestra, or the fact that you're spending a lot of time as chair of its board of trustees. Balancing conflicting expectations is central to your success. Playing your multiple roles to the benefit of the organization's long-term future is crucial. Indeed, the wise CEO does not simply *play* these roles at all; he or she *lives* them.

Starting at Ground Zero

But before we go too far waxing philosophically about your impressive new significance or your aura, remember—you have a job to do. So roll up your sleeves and get down to work. Recognize that you've entered new territory and that first and foremost you are on a fact-finding mission. The important first phase of any new job is that of discovery.

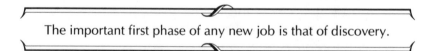

The important first phase of any new job is that of discovery.

Whoever filled the job before you operated on certain assumptions, many of which may now be obsolete or simply unfounded. It's time to question those assumptions and to dig for facts. Think of yourself as a detective sorting through clues or an archeologist with a pick but not much of a map. As Lee Iacocca advises, "During the first couple of weeks in a new job, you look for telltale signs." You won't find these in the chairman's office. There's just spit and polish there, and well-rehearsed presentations. So move around.

Most important, get to know your people. Many new chief executives allow themselves to get too caught up in paperwork and ceremony. There is no time like the present to set your own agenda, steering clear of the routines that others may try to set for your job. It's time especially to have one-on-one meetings, and not just with your own direct reports. A cynical observation that's made the rounds for years is that the day a person becomes chief executive is the last day he or she will hear the unvarnished truth. From then on facts will be filtered, and presentations will be carefully censored. But success can only come through a clear connection to reality, so this is the time to get a firm grasp on that reality.

Think back to your first job as first-line manager. You needed to know two things: what was happening, *actually* happening, in your sphere of responsibility, and whom you could count on for help. Your needs today are no different.

> The basic qualities of leadership apply to all levels of management, and the first-line manager, like the CEO, sets an example for others.

Not all new chief executives start out by meeting with their people. Harold Geneen, former ITT chief executive, describes how he spent his first week or so going through reams of paper, poring over figures. He too was seeking reality, but his approach did not help him gain an understanding of his people. Instead, it distanced him from them just at the time when they most wanted to know what he was like. No doubt they decided anyway, but based on the inhospitable signals he was giving.

In contrast, when Marisa Bellisario became managing director and CEO of the Italian state-owned Italtel organization in 1981, she sized up her people as follows:

> The first thing I look for when I take on a new job and the first thing I did at Italtel was to try to get the best top-level people I could to help manage the company. I chose a team of highly professional managers both from outside the company and within. . . . The most important part of the solution is to find the right executives. You can make changes from the top, but it is quite im-

possible to make them at the bottom without the right leadership.

Though the chief executive occupies a special position at the top of the organization, there are many ways in which that job and the job of a first-line manager are similar. Both require leadership. Leaders (and they exist at all levels) know instinctively that success depends not so much on themselves as on others. One of their traits is to recognize the positive attributes of their people and then build upon those strengths. Because the behavior of most human beings is set very early in life, leaders do not expect their people to change radically. But they do try to help them grow, through giving them increasingly larger responsibilities. Leaders learn how much they can delegate by constantly testing the limits of their people. Leaders never shirk from decision making, but neither do they insist on making all the decisions. Letting others make decisions is one way to test their limits and to stretch them. I'm convinced that the basic qualities of leadership apply to all levels of management, and the first-line manager, like the CEO, sets an example for others, builds leadership support, and helps to cultivate other leaders throughout his or her career.

Chapter Three

Decision Making: Does Rambo Have It Right?

In American culture, decisiveness is a virtue. Those who shrink from making decisions become the butt of jokes. They are the henpecked husbands, the wishy-washy, the Caspar Milquetoasts of the world. In contrast, that world-class media icon J. R. Ewing of *Dallas* fame never flinched from a decision. Unencumbered by morals, J. R. would unblinkingly double-cross a friend, steal from his mother, or bed a beautiful regulatory commissioner. No matter how distasteful, J. R. would do whatever had to be done. "Participatory decision making? That stuff doesn't make it in the oil patch. Except maybe for that wimp Cliff Barnes. And who needs him?"

This attitude spills over into many corporate cultures, where macho is the preferred attitude. You might hear: "The hell with getting the whole group together. I'm paid to decide, and by God this is what I have decided to do. Now let's make it happen." When it doesn't happen (and often it doesn't), you might hear: "Maybe I need to fire a few people around here to get my point across. Say, did you see the new Rambo movie? I really *like* that guy!"

Why keep people informed and enlist their input? Let them do their own thing. The spirit of Ollie North and the ghost of Bill Casey still permeate many corporate boardrooms and managers' offices. And why not? To make an omelet you have to break a few eggs. Who needs a task force for that? History honors explorers, pioneers, risk takers, individualists. You would search the great capitals of the world in vain for a monument to any committee.

On the other hand you might find quite a few ruins of earlier nations and civilizations brought to destruction by one-man rule. So maybe there are two sides to this issue of decision making.

Of course, most businesses are not run like Ewing Oil (though thousands of real family businesses are torn apart by rivalries among family members). But in every organization there is the need to know just who is authorized to make what kinds of decisions. Successful companies are neither dictatorships nor democracies. In the best-run companies, decision-making authority is widely but carefully dispersed. The level to which decision making is delegated depends on three factors: the significance of the decision to the organization, the level at which needed information is available to make the right decision, and the perceived judgment of the person who will make the decision.

The macho man quoted above is right about one thing: Managers *are* paid to make decisions. But they're also paid to think about whether the decision is theirs to make. The manager who

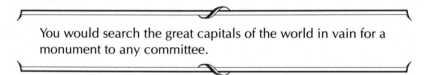

You would search the great capitals of the world in vain for a monument to any committee.

hoards decision-making authority is just as dangerous as the one who shuns it.

A new first-line manager may hesitate to decide an issue for fear of usurping his or her manager's prerogative—or worse, for fear of taking a personal risk. "What will happen if I make the wrong decision?" he or she may wonder. "Maybe I'd better check." In most cases communication with the supervising manager will set the bounds of the first-line manager's decision-making authority.

Management training programs often suggest that a three-level hierarchy of authority be established at the outset: "Which kinds of decisions can I make without telling anyone? Which kinds do I have to communicate upward? And which kinds am I not allowed to make?" While this is an appropriate framework, reality is rarely neat enough to fit any frame. So until a first-line manager and his or her supervisor have worked together long enough to be comfortable with each other, it is wise to err on the side of overcommunication. Once a smooth relationship has been developed, the decision framework will become clearer and less ambiguous. Such a relationship, however, requires trust on both sides, as do CEOs' relationships.

Deciding Who Decides

Decision making, like learning to ski downhill, requires courage. But eventually it becomes a habit. Routine decisions are made swiftly; difficult ones are made more slowly and with care.

Still, habits can become addictions. Decision junkies, those managers who delegate the heavy lifting but keep to themselves the authority to decide what is to be lifted, can wreck any organization—in the short term by making wrong decisions, as they surely will; and over the long term by driving good people away, hence inflicting permanent damage. Decision junkies illustrate John Dewey's claim that the brain is an organ of last resort. Too busy to think about the context and ultimate consequences of decisions, such managers go about deciding through knee-jerk responses. The question they fail to ask themselves is the question that should precede any decision: "Is this decision mine to make?"

Of course, now that you're sitting in the CEO's chair, you're entitled to do—and decide—just about anything you want. After all, you run the place. How better to ensure consistency than to make every decision yourself? Doesn't quality come from attention to the nitty-gritty? Doesn't your organization (and every organization) need consistency?

If there were a Management Hall of Shame, it would be filled with statues of those who dedicated their business lives, and their every waking moment, to minutiae—to deciding *everything*. Walter J. Connolly, Jr., former CEO of The Bank of New England, ruled his fiefdom with an iron hand. Autocratic, temperamental, inconsistent, and demanding, he earned the acronym WWW for his "leadership" style: Whatever Walter Wants.

What he got, according to an article in a leading business magazine, was a group of terrified yes-men. At senior management meetings he would humiliate one top executive after another and frighten them all. Eventually, in early 1990, the bank's board of directors ousted him. By that time, however, the bank had been seized by the federal government.

An examination revealed $1.2 billion worth of bad real estate loans. Because Connolly had personally wooed real estate developers and made loans to them without consulting the bank's

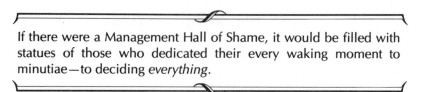

If there were a Management Hall of Shame, it would be filled with statues of those who dedicated their every waking moment to minutiae—to deciding *everything*.

lending officers, there was no question that Connolly had been decisive. Decisive to a fault. Decisive to the end—his own end and the bank's. He had wrecked the bank by consistently failing to ask the simple, essential question: "Is this decision mine to make?" Decision junkies occasionally rise to the top, but few stay there. There are other questions essential to good decision making:

"Who has the information needed for this decision?"
"Who will be affected?"
"Who else needs to know?"
"What will be the long-term consequences of this decision?"

But most important:

"Who should make this decision?"

By developing the habit of asking these questions, you can facilitate decision making throughout the organization and improve the quality of the decisions as well.

The usual answer to the question "Who should make this decision?" is "The person most qualified to make it." That is, the person who is most informed, especially about possible consequences. Unless those who must live with the consequences of a decision have a large say in making it, trouble may lie ahead. The reason is that getting a decision made is never enough. Even brilliant decisions may fail in implementation. In football, a good call by the quarterback may fail in execution through an incomplete pass. In the game of business, the corporate quarterback may fail to designate a receiver or, worse, may hold onto the ball and get sacked. So still another question must be asked:

"Who will implement the decision, and on what schedule?"

Finally, there is need for follow-through. Because human beings are imperfect and business is complex, there's a need to know that the decision has in fact been implemented and a need to observe its consequences, which are often not quite what was intended. But unless the decision is in fact implemented, you'll never know its effect. Good decisions and good intentions are not the same thing. When Corning's CEO James Houghton trumpeted his corporatewide message of quality, nothing happened. It was only after he began to hold specific people accountable for results that results began to happen. Until then, he says, his people "thought it was the flavor of the month."

The massive inertia of large organizations can be dealt with only by massive and sustained attack. Without specific and documented executors of decisions, the problem the decision was supposed to address will keep coming back. So if you don't want to be haunted by your decisions, make certain you know exactly who is responsible for making them happen.

Finally, there is the following rule: Establish a method and criteria for follow-through.

Not Just the Facts, Ma'am

As Peter Drucker pointed out twenty-five years ago in *The Effective Executive*, a decision is a choice between alternatives but rarely a choice between right and wrong. It's much more often "a choice between two courses of action neither of which is provably more nearly right than the other." Nor is it based merely on facts. In real life, a fact is often in the eye of the beholder. Decisions, on the other hand, are largely based on opinions.

One of my early mentors claimed, with little exaggeration, that every decision is emotional. Clearly, the decisions you make rest heavily on your assumptions. Differences in opinion as to which way a decision should go are usually based on the differing assumptions that people hold. So, it's vital to test your assumptions before racing to a decision. But assumptions do not exist in a vacuum. Instead, they are usually influenced by emotion, and emotions are based on values and beliefs.

In 1983, Gordon Donaldson and Jay Lorsch published findings of their research on decision making at the top. In each company, they studied how individual beliefs affected the way corporate managers thought about internal management issues and the relationship of these issues to strategic choices. They concluded that these beliefs weighed heavily on the ultimate outcome of decisions. One top manager, for example, might have a deep-seated belief in teamwork, saying to himself, "We are all one big interactive team of 40,000 people." Another might say, "We must be willing to delegate responsibility to our separate units," each of which might operate in its distinctive way. Neither belief is right or wrong. In some organizations one approach will work well, and in another it may not work at all.

Decision-Making Do's and Don'ts

The art of decision making has more to do with effectiveness than with theory. And despite the many words written about decisions since Chester I. Barnard wrote *The Functions of the Executive* in 1938, Barnard should have the last word when he says the following:

> The fine art of executive decision consists in not deciding questions that are not now pertinent, in not deciding prematurely, in not making decisions that cannot be made effective, and in not making decisions that others should make.

But it also consists in *making* those decisions that *must* be made when they *should* be made.

Following Barnard's advice is never easy, nor are the kinds of decisions that force their way to the top in times of uncertainty. Robert Crandall, chairman of American Airlines, explains it well:

Most people at big corporations are rarely certain of what they ought to do. The management of these enterprises is a process of balancing what is always competing evidence as to the proper course of action, and weighing that, and betting on the side of the most probable outcome.

If it were clear what should be done, these jobs wouldn't be nearly so hard.

Retailing giant Ralph Lazarus, former chairman and CEO of Federated Department Stores, Inc., gives this advice:

It's essential that *whatever decisions you make, you make with conviction.* You're not going to be a dynamic leader if you can't do that. In this field, correct decisions have to be based on fact, but facts are not enough; you need spirit and soul. You won't be a real leader unless you fully believe your decisions will not only be acceptable but will be enthusiastically received by the thousands of people in the rank and file.

Lazarus illustrates his point by telling an anecdote about a buyer at the original Lazarus family store in Columbus, Ohio, many years ago. The buyer came across a job lot of fine Oriental rugs and, knowing quality, he bought the whole lot. Lazarus's father, then general merchandising manager, saw no market in Columbus for such expensive floor coverings and "just hit the ceiling!" But the buyer's instincts carried the day. "Let me tell you," Lazarus says, "Columbus bought more Oriental rugs in those two weeks than it had consumed in the previous ten years! That's what conviction and enthusiasm will do."

Listen to Yourself

To make the right decisions, you need facts. Unshakable facts. You need self-confidence. And a conviction that the decision is yours to make. You need to confer with other people and to inform still others. But the really difficult decisions require something even more: guts. Not just the guts to make the decision, for often you will find that the only place to look for guidance *is* your gut. At times your mind will be saying no while your guts are whispering yes.

In the early 1980s, Harry Levinson and Stuart Rosenthal interviewed six of the most capable chief executives in the United States. These leaders were deeply involved, emotionally committed, and "bound to the organizations they served and directed." In the end, "the single note of self-criticism struck by all of the leaders was that they hadn't followed their intuition and instincts as assiduously as they should have."

This has been my experience, too. There have been times when my instincts drove me toward a decision, but I was talked out of it by highly logical, irrefutable arguments. Whenever I followed my instincts on a tough call, my decision turned out to be right. And whenever I yielded to others' objections, I often later regretted that I had turned away from what I originally thought was right.

In this connection, the Reverend John Cavanaugh, a former

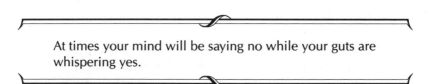

At times your mind will be saying no while your guts are whispering yes.

president of the University of Notre Dame, gave the following advice to his successor:

> When you make a decision, however large or small, do not ask "what is the easy thing to do?" Or "what will cost the least money?" Or "what will make me the most loved or popular by those affected by the decision?" Just ask what is the *right* decision, all things considered. Once you have made that judgment, and you'll make it better once you have been burned a few times, then just do it, decide it, no matter how difficult it is, no matter how costly, no matter how unpopular. In the long run, whatever the immediate uproar or inconveniences, people, your people, will respect you for following your

conscience, for doing what you thought right, even though they do not agree with you.

More important, you'll respect yourself.

Because the tough decisions require consultation with your inner self, they often take time to make. Signals from your brain are interfering with messages from your viscera, and internal confusion reigns. Whenever this happens, it is exactly the wrong time to make the decision. Instead, go jogging. Have sex. Go to a movie. Read a book. Play with your kids or grandchildren. Or do something really unusual—like taking your spouse to dinner at the most elegant restaurant you can find. In other words, get away from the issue by finding some pleasant distraction, and simply decide *not* to decide for a few days. Whenever you do this, you will find that the decision is somehow being made in your subconscious. When left alone, the pieces magically fall together. And you'll wake up one morning completely rested and supremely confident about what to do.

The lessons from this discussion? Never make decisions that are not yours to make. Don't make your own decisions too quickly. And, for those mind-boggling dilemmas that keep you awake at night, never, never, never attack them frontally.

Finally, don't forget to keep people fully informed. Remember, even if your decision is a home run, you still need to touch all the bases.

Chapter Four

Climbing the Learning Curve

When you first started work, you probably had no idea of how much you would eventually need to know. New employees often enter a company with very specialized knowledge in a particular area such as accounting or engineering. And this may be all the knowledge that is necessary to successfully carry out many entry-level positions.

The opinion has often been expressed that a liberal arts education, with its more general overview, is of little use to a young man or woman trying to get started in the competitive world of business. When your job is to map out an electrical circuit or to audit a business ledger, what difference does it make that you know the difference between Beowulf and Thomas Wolfe, Manet and Monet, Einstein and Gertrude Stein? And for the most part, as you began your career you may have been right to question the value of such knowledge in the face of your everyday work responsibilities. But as you begin to move up the ladder of leadership, you notice that your specialized knowledge, while still useful, begins to have less prominence in how successfully you fulfill your job.

Effective management does not hinge on a restricted field of knowledge, no matter how expert you are in it. The higher you rise in the corporation, the more encompassing becomes your view. So a liberal arts education can be very useful to the CEO—the scientific method for analysis; history for perspective; geography for understanding an increasingly interconnected world economy. And don't forget literature, with its emphasis on the human condition. J. Douglas Brown, dean emeritus of Princeton University, once claimed that Shakespeare is the CEO's best mentor.

Still, as a new CEO—or a new manager at any level—you need to learn many specific, even mundane, things about your business and your people. To get started on the learning curve, you have no choice but to rely on your people, even while you are trying to assess their capabilities and earn their support.

At the same time, the momentum of your new responsibilities drives you forward. You may have the feeling that you're in the driver's seat of a foreign racing car speeding on an unfamiliar track. There is also a nagging worry that you may be on the wrong track. Curiously, there is also a sense of déjà vu: You have suffered the symptoms of the new job syndrome before.

In an interview with Harvard Business School professor John J. Gabarro, a divisional general manager eighteen months into his job recalled his feelings:

> You have to learn about [your] people and their capabilities awfully fast, and that's the trickiest thing to do. At first you are afraid to do anything for fear of upsetting the apple cart. The problem is you have to keep the business *running* while you *learn* about it.

Worse, the demands of the business, or those you place on yourself, may suggest that there's no time to stop and reflect on what is happening, no time even to slow down. You may be tempted to try to change the tire on that figurative racing car yourself, leaving your crew to wonder about their roles. And about your judgment.

In any new job you simply must make the time to chart your course and especially to get to know your people. And, just as important, for them to get to know you. Peter G. Scotese, former CEO of Springs Industries, says this: "You can have a very good batting average on judging people if you spend enough time with them. . . . [I]f you are willing to pay the price of that amount of time and effort, you will rarely go wrong." He offers the following advice for the beginning of any assignment:

> I cannot think of any device that will attract someone to a new person more quickly than just sitting down and

just saying, "I'm new here; I don't know very much and maybe not a damn thing about the company; you have an important role here, so would you please help me; tell me about *yourself*; tell me about the strengths and the weaknesses in the organization as *you* perceive them. I may or may not do something about it, and I may even see it differently, but I have got to have as much knowledge of the operation from where you sit as I can get." For someone just coming into the situation, this is essential. . . . [O]nce you finish with the key people, you can put together a jigsaw that gives you a fairly good impression going in of what the company . . . is all about.

Not all the pieces of that jigsaw puzzle can be found within the organization. To learn what the company is *really* about, you'll need to meet with customers, suppliers, and others—but first and foremost with customers.

According to Charles Lazarus, chief executive of Toys'R'Us, it's all very simple: "You just listen to the customers, then act on what they tell you." In many organizations, however, it is not so

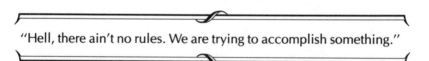

"Hell, there ain't no rules. We are trying to accomplish something."

simple. Rules and procedures—each established for a reason that made sense at the time—combine to create obstacles. Donald Coggiola, senior vice-president of Policy Management Systems, describes a client company's approval process as "giant pools of peanut butter we have to swim through."

No one knows the depth and viscosity of a company's bureaucracy better than its customers. The internal walls between functions and the "that's not my department's responsibility" attitude may be hidden from top management or even defended by some of its members. So, the view from outside is critically important to gaining an understanding of how the organization works.

The CEO of a major multinational firm once complained to

me about his company's own bureaucracy. "You'd think," he said, "that I could get whatever I wanted done. I've got strong people around me, and that's good. But they can come up with twenty reasons why my ideas won't work."

Thomas Alva Edison was once asked by a new staff member at his "invention factory" in West Orange, New Jersey, about rules. "Hell, there ain't no rules," Edison replied. "We are trying to accomplish something."

Today, there is virtually no organization that can make such a claim, if for no other reason than the proliferation of government regulations. But there are probably more internally generated rules, in most companies, than externally imposed ones, and every manager must work hard to decrease their number to the irreducible minimum. You'll learn which ones irritate your customers only by asking them. And listening hard.

Developing "Outside" Vision

Some years ago, Xerox prided itself on its ability to ship copy machines from its factories in only two weeks. To its customers, however, the important issue was how quickly the copiers could be successfully *installed* and accurately billed. Xerox's newly elected chief executive, Paul Allaire, described the situation as a real embarrassment and handed the problem to an experienced manager, who solved it by creating a team of people from all departments involved.

"You can't get people to focus only on the bottom line," Allaire says. "You have to give them an objective like 'satisfy the customer' that everyone can relate to. It's the only way to break down those barriers and get people from different functions working together." Like many others, this problem would not even have surfaced without direct customer feedback. Most of the self-inflicted problems of my own career have been caused by looking at things from an internal perspective. Finally, I learned my lesson: You've got to develop "outside eyes."

To the new CEO, reading is essential. Industry studies, market research reports, customer-satisfaction surveys, focus-group responses—all these and more must be scanned by the incoming chief, who may need to mete out assignments to seek information that is not available. In short, the new chief executive must become steeped in industry and market knowledge, only a small part of which may be available internally. Nevertheless, a lot of information *is* available, only for the asking.

In the early stage of a management assignment, perhaps more than at any other, listening skills are critical. Executives vary greatly in their ability to listen. Jacques Maisonrouge, former président directeur général of IBM World Trade Corporation, observes of good managers he has met: "They know how to listen . . . and when they understand more quickly than others, they are discreet enough not to show it." Instead, you need to become what Charlotte L. Beers, former chairman and CEO of Tatham-Laird & Kudner, calls an "earnest listener." Of an earlier position at J. Walter Thompson, she says the following:

> I sure wasn't known for [listening] at Thompson, where I was more of an impatient catalyst, making things happen. There I felt the *worst* thing I could do was to listen too long! But here [at TLK] I *had* to hear what people were saying and weren't saying, so I spent a lot of time listening, trying to understand where they felt short of talent or self-conscious or uncertain, to see if I had strengths to fill in the gaps. And, if I didn't, to try to figure out how we could fill them in.

Now, as new chairwoman and CEO of Ogilvy & Mather Worldwide, she is no doubt listening earnestly once more. The early stage is a time to listen especially to members of the top team—and to suspend judgment about them. By spending enough time with them and observing their actions and results, and the way they seek or share credit, you'll get to know them. In the beginning, however, they need time to get comfortable with you, to learn to trust you.

The fact is that you are being judged by them from the signals you send, wittingly or otherwise. There is but one opportunity to make a first impression, and you have already made yours. If your actions are consistent, that first impression will be confirmed. Inconsistent actions can drive a wedge between you and them, and inconsistencies between words and actions will drive a very deep wedge.

A study by Harvard professor John J. Gabarro of differences between successful and unsuccessful managers emphasizes the importance of team building: "A prevalent characteristic of failed successions was that the manager was viewed by subordinates and superiors as having failed to develop a cohesive management team by the end of his first twelve months." In some cases the managers who failed had chosen not to work with their direct reports as a *group*, but rather dealt with them individually or through formal communications. In other cases they failed to develop effective teams through "an unwillingness or inability to resolve conflicts already existing within the management group."

A second reason for failure was that managers made ill-conceived changes that did not work, either because the changes were based on inadequate or wrong diagnoses of problems, or because their teams did not support them; hence the changes suffered in implementation. This comprehensive study, ranging across several levels of management, suggests the following advice: Don't make too many changes too quickly. Remember, you are on the steep slope of the learning curve.

Diagnosis of problems in a business setting can be as complex as in the field of medicine, and actions based on flawed diagnoses can be just as disastrous. A little-known medical adjective, "iatrogenic," describes a condition inadvertently brought about by a physician's treatment. In any complex organization a change or two *here* may trigger a problem or two *there*; unforeseen difficulties

> Don't make too many changes too quickly. You are on the steep slope of the learning curve.

cascade down or spread across the organization. Impulsive actions made in good faith by an unseasoned manager or CEO can create problems far more serious than those the actions were intended to cure. Beware, therefore, the onset of "CEOgenic" maladies—dysfunctions caused by ill-conceived decisions at the top!

"The Fault, Dear Brutus, Is Not in Our Stars"

The diagnosis of organizational malfunctions simply takes time, even if the company is in critical financial shape. It is made no easier by defensive managers who tend to point innocent fingers at other departments or, predictably, to lay the blame for poor results on external conditions.

It is important, of course, to understand outside influences that are negatively affecting operations, and we all know that list: a slowed economy, unreasonable government regulations, unseasonable weather, unfavorable currency-exchange rates, unfair foreign competition, and on and on. But it might be productive to label these tentatively as excuses and go on quickly to the process of discovering the internal causes, the only ones you can do anything about.

When Toshihiko Yamashita became president in 1977 of the giant Matsushita Electric Co., Ltd., profits were growing in only two of its forty-eight operating divisions. Oddly enough, the only healthy divisions operated in mature industries, producing electric irons and storage batteries. "We were in trouble," Yamashita observed, "perhaps terminally ill. . . . Matsushita had become sluggish, overweight, myopic. Worst of all, the patient was so complacent that he didn't recognize his own mid-life crisis." The lifeblood of Matsushita's divisional organization was supposed to be the autonomy of the division directors, but some, he said, "were more concerned . . . about pleasing headquarters than asserting their independence." In most divisions, decisions were not being made.

Yamashita approached his challenge in an interesting way: He studied the two successful divisions and the reasons for their success. He also looked, elsewhere, for important decisions that needed to be made but instead were stuck in the company's phlegmatic bureaucracy.

One of these decisions concerned whether to press forward with Matsushita's VHS version of the VCR (of which only a prototype model existed) in the face of the fierce competition presented by Sony's Betamax version, which was already enjoying some success in the large U.S. market. He decided to take the risk, the "rash gamble," as he later called it, and his decision paid off— but only after he had mobilized key people from many divisions, who "ate, drank, and slept . . . VCRs" for months. As a result, Matsushita triumphed over Sony and garnered "a lucrative market share."

"There'll Be Some Changes Made"

When Lee Iacocca became president of Chrysler Corp. in 1978, it had just announced its largest loss in the history of the company. Arriving at headquarters, he found three dozen vice-presidents, each with his own turf, and soon learned that the company was running out of cash. Worse, he said, "Nobody at Chrysler seemed to understand that interaction among the different functions is absolutely critical. People in engineering and manufacturing almost have to be sleeping together. These guys weren't even flirting!"

To overcome the entrenched Chrysler bureaucracy, changes in key positions had to be made—and soon. Iacocca recalls: "There was so much to do and so little time! I had to eliminate the thirty-five little duchies. I had to bring some cohesion and unity into the company. I had to get rid of the many people who didn't know what they were doing. I had to replace them by finding guys with experience who could move fast."

Yamashita remembers his first days at Matsushita this way: "Complacency started at the top. . . . The company had become a huge bureaucracy—layers of managers, countless meetings, and slow reaction time." For the first year, Yamashita worked with, and around, the three executive vice-presidents (each older than he) to whom the division heads reported. Finally, he made the painful decision, especially so in Japan, to force them out of the company.

The founder of the company, Konosuke Matsushita, then serving as executive advisor, was concerned about the effect on the new president of the criticism Yamashita was receiving in the press for this and other drastic decisions. One day he brought a framed piece of his own Chinese calligraphy to the office. The message inscribed for the new president was "great patience," a quality needed for successful leadership at any level, and especially at the beginning of an assignment.

Still, few chief executives are known for their patience. And a case can be made for taking some early actions to help define themselves in the minds of their people.

For example, on his first day as chairman of Alcoa in June 1987, Paul O'Neill identified safety as Alcoa's highest priority. Not profit, not market share, not quality, but safety. His reasoning rested not only on the value and importance he places on human life, but on the clear connections between safety and quality, and between quality and success in the market.

He took other symbolic actions as well by insisting that company-paid memberships in country clubs be limited to those clubs that did not practice discrimination and by divesting himself of his limousine and driver. These symbolic actions spoke louder than any words he could have chosen.

Leaders at all levels might benefit from reflecting on these words by Ralph Waldo Emerson: "What you are stands over you . . . and thunders so that I cannot hear what you say."

Chapter Five

Planning:
The Job You Can't Delegate

As CEO the most difficult yet most important part of your job is to position your company for the future. To do so requires a commitment to change and a vision firmly rooted in reality. The responsibility for that vision rests squarely on your shoulders, for the future success of your enterprise is one of the few things that can never be delegated. This was not always thought to be so. In the decades immediately following World War II corporate planning departments grew in size and number. But the shocks of unprecedented global competition and the merger-and-acquisition binge of the 1980s caused many chief executives to take a hands-on role in planning.

Despite its importance, planning is one of the least popular and most misunderstood parts of managing, simply because it is so often done poorly. The seat-of-the-pants CEO may gather the top team together and use the occasion to expound on corporate philosophy. Or the CEO can go around the room collecting opinions, thinking all the time that planning is taking place. Or, time can be misspent by simply updating last year's plan. Such misuses of the top team's time have given planning a bad name.

In contrast, successful planning is based on a systematic approach that is bought into by members of your top management team. The particular approach chosen—and there are dozens—is less important than its ownership by each of your team members. When you finish, it had better be *their* plan, not just yours.

Good planning starts with facts. These must be clearly distinguished from half-baked opinions. Before beginning any planning session, you'll need an information base composed of what Harold Geneen, former chief executive of ITT, called unshakable facts: "No matter what you think, try shaking it to be sure." You'll also need an agreed upon set of assumptions, for otherwise the plan will rest on a shifting foundation. And unless everyone present participates, you won't even know whether your people have bought into those assumptions. So spend time probing their points of view.

The ultimate purpose of planning is to answer this question: "What business should we be in?" Yet the heads of many companies are uncertain as to what businesses they actually *are* in. Consultants report the frequent lack of hard answers, even at the top, to such simple questions as these: "Who are our customers? Why do they buy? Who are really our major competitors, and what are their strengths?"

Unless such questions can be answered with confidence, any attempt at serious planning will be an even more humbling experience than it should be. (And, at best, it's humbling enough.) For these reasons, you should give specific homework assignments to members of your top team. You'll need at the start to thoroughly discuss the planning process itself. *Before* launching into it. Each member of the team should in turn hold discussions with his or her people, and so on down the line. Time should be allowed for communications to cascade down. And for suggestions to bubble up.

Harvesting "Intellectual Capital"

About ten years ago I asked a number of CEOs and management scholars this question: "What is the essential contribution of a chief executive?" The most interesting response came from Lawrence Fouraker, then dean of the Harvard Business School, who replied: "Intellectual capital." This phrase, then new to me, is now being heard more and more often.

Defined by Hugh McDonald of I.C.L., the U.K. computer manufacturer, as the "knowledge that exists in an organization that can be used to create differential advantage," intellectual capital is even more than that: It is the sum total of the useful knowledge of your employees and your customers. Far more valuable to your business than even your material and financial resources, intellectual capital represents the raw material for a successful strategic plan. Therefore, the essential preparation for planning is the gathering of facts, perceptions, insights, and differing perspectives.

According to Sören Olsson, president of Apple Computer Europe, Inc., "In the information age, it's not just more data that counts, it's how information is accessed and how it is used. It's taking advantage of the knowledge resources within the organization, wherever they reside." And outside the organization as well, I would add.

The effective CEO develops numerous sources of information, so you should be seeking out not only facts but informed opinion. In 1963, shortly after Arthur ("Punch") Ochs Sulzberger became chief executive of The New York Times Company and publisher of *The New York Times*, one of his colleagues said this: "I've seen him absorbing advice almost the way a sponge sucks up water. What I don't see . . . is where does the squeezing process begin and what is the factor that starts to force some of the water that's been absorbed out. I know this process he has of going to all sorts of people, listening to all sorts of different opinions. . . ."

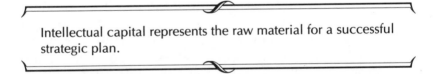

Intellectual capital represents the raw material for a successful strategic plan.

The alert chief executive listens especially hard for alarms. Some years ago, while on a trip to California to improve his company's mortgage business there, Robert G. Schwartz, president, chairman, and CEO of Metropolitan Life Insurance, was told that the reason for declining mortgage activity at MetLife was that the company was too slow. Schwartz inquired why and was told the following: "You take the time to look at what you buy." Rather than speeding up the process, which many would have done, Schwartz reflected on this bit of intellectual capital. As a result, his company continued its conservative approach. In contrast, the Equitable's assets went into a precipitous decline in the late 1980s, and Executive Life failed in 1991—both because an emphasis on sales volume took precedence over prudence.

The effective squeezing of intellectual capital through the planning sieve provides the basis for decisions that can shape the future. Scarce resources can often be freed up by answering these important questions: What businesses are we now in that we should *not* be in? Should those parts of the business be sold, milked for profit, or simply abandoned? Peter Drucker describes what he calls systematic abandonment as the sloughing off of yesterday, and he emphasizes its importance if there is to be a successful tomorrow.

It is your task as chief executive to put the ever-changing resource of intellectual capital to use. Yesterday's assumptions won't work even for the most successful, entrenched businesses. Every enterprise must reposition itself for a changing future.

In his classic book, *The Practice of Management*, written in the early 1950s, Drucker held up Sears, Roebuck & Company as one of the greatest commercial success stories in America. And so it clearly was at that time. Around the turn of the century, then-CEO Julius Rosenwald had recognized the unserved rural market and developed a superb mail-order organization to serve it. But then came the Model T.

In 1918, Henry Ford read in a letter from a farmer's wife in Georgia, "Your car lifted us out of the mud. It brought joy into our lives. We loved every rattle in its bones. . . ." With the farmer out of the mud and no longer dependent on mail-order catalogs, Sears's new CEO, General Robert E. Wood, began to build a network of urban retail stores that succeeded for decades. With characteristic prescience, Drucker ended his account with these words: "Sears may have to think through what its business is, where its markets are, and what innovations are needed."

Sadly, in later years this advice was ignored. Sears lost not only its dominant position in retailing but its direction, as did many other retail chains and department stores in general.

Meanwhile, in the small town of Bentonville, Arkansas, a plain-thinking man named Sam Walton envisioned a vast small-town market for quality goods at discounted prices. By 1992, Wal-Mart had created nearly 2,000 stores employing over a third of a million people, while a battered, shrunken Sears, no longer the nation's largest retailer, was struggling to understand what business it should be in. At the same time, Kmart was breathing down

Wal-Mart's neck—with Target Stores coming up fast, already beating out Kmart in sales per square foot. Other retailing niches had been filled by superstores, warehouse clubs, and other innovative retail organizations, while the traditional retail industry was in shambles and its once proud merchandisers deep in debt.

In Pursuit of the Master Stroke

Incremental improvements to one's business can come through effective planning. The *kaizen* concept of continuous improvement is claimed by Masaaki Imai to be the single most important concept in Japanese management and the key to Japan's competitive success. Yet more is needed—*much* more.

According to Richard A. Zimmerman, chairman and CEO of Hershey Foods Corporation:

> In the best CEOs, planning is built into the psyche. Yet despite that disciplined approach, good chief executives never lose sight of taking that master stroke. There is always something out there they are constantly looking for and asking themselves, "How can we achieve this, how can we get to that next point?" So while you always need to be moving along incrementally, you still need that master stroke that can reposition your company.

What *is* that master stroke? It is your duty to be constantly on the lookout for external changes that offer new opportunities, even small ones. And it is not only major demographic or technological changes such as the mass distribution of the automobile that create market opportunities. For example, Hershey perceived a new product possibility during the 1991 Persian Gulf War and met it by creating the Desert Bar, a milk chocolate confection capable of withstanding high temperatures. Despite Hershey's speed in developing this product, the Department of Defense ordered not a single bar. So in the days of patriotic fervor following that war, the Desert Bar became a consumer item attractive to those who had earlier purchased yellow ribbons and American flags.

Employees deep within the organization often have ideas about new products or services but simply haven't been asked. A dramatic example of the power of such ideas occurred in 1986 when Walt Disney Co. ran a contest which asked its employees for suggestions for new company opportunities. The idea most frequently suggested was a chain of retail outlets for Disney products to be sold outside its theme parks. By 1991, there were 100 such stores open in the United States, and plans were underway to expand them into Europe and Japan.

Long-term customers, often taken for granted, represent another source of ideas. They may know of a new product or service they need. Failing to get it from your organization, they will find it elsewhere. It is the building up and sifting through of the organization's intellectual capital that transforms this raw material into a company's vision. The CEO who fails to call on this resource unwittingly yields opportunity to current competitors or encourages the creation of new ones.

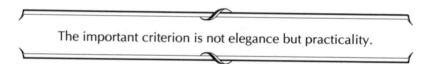

The important criterion is not elegance but practicality.

In searching for the master stroke and in defining the vision of the company, the important criterion is not elegance but practicality. Microsoft chairman William H. Gates 3rd, the Harvard dropout who became a self-made billionaire in his early thirties, achieved his position in the industry not by developing elegant software packages but by making computers easier to use. H. Wayne Huizenga, chairman of Blockbuster Entertainment Corporation, decided to serve the massive market of home movie watchers by offering convenience, variety, and value in tape rentals. One simple innovation was to allow customers to keep the tapes two days rather than just overnight. Earlier, Huizenga had created his first billion-dollar company, Waste Management, by acquiring dozens of independent cartage companies and building a giant business on the unglamorous base of garbage collection.

These and other successful companies were guided to success by CEOs who developed a simple vision and communicated it in words so unmistakably clear that the course to the future could be followed.

Fine-Tuning the Vision

Vision, however, is never enough. To succeed there must also be a plan. Start-up companies that are based on entrepreneurial ideas can flourish in their early years by probing various market opportunities. But eventually they need focus.

ASK Computer Systems, for example, the largest public company founded and run by a woman, began very modestly by applying time-sharing technology to the management of kids' paper routes. Sandra L. Kurtzig began the operation in the second bedroom of her house because, she said, "I couldn't even afford a garage." Later, after applying computers to advanced manufacturing applications, ASK began to carve out a niche for itself, but by 1976 it found itself badly overcommitted.

Realizing that ASK couldn't be all things to all companies, Kurtzig began to define her competition, which at the time was fragmented and confusing. "Being part of such a confused market made it difficult for us to get a clear fix on competitors or predict what direction the industry would take. It did, however, provide the opportunity for a company like ASK to stake out a quick claim, then grow large and fast enough to make it difficult for any challengers to succeed. That is precisely what we did," she said. By continuously focusing and refocusing ASK, she built a company whose annual revenues in 1990 approached $400 million. By planning, Sandra Kurtzig took charge of her company's future.

Most studies of leadership define as one of its elements the act of taking responsibility. In the 1940s, Chester Barnard described responsibility as an emotional condition that "gives an individual a sense of acute dissatisfaction" when he or she does not take it.

Having become CEO, you realize (or soon will) that you cannot take charge of everything, at least in a hands-on way. But by calling on your company's intellectual capital and by getting your top team to help you plan, *really* plan, you can begin to take charge of the company's future. As CEO it's easy and even tempting to take charge of all the wrong things, tasks that can be handled as well, or better, by others. But if you don't take charge of your company's future, there's no one else who will—or can. Other than your competitors.

Chapter Six

Those Lonesome CEO Blues

Is it really lonely at the top, or is this a myth? Your schedule is packed with meetings. A line of people forms outside your office. There are a dozen phone calls to return. For days you've been trying to find time for a haircut. Surrounded by people, you're told there's a reporter on one line and a lawyer on another. How can you possibly be lonely? Your job is a series of interruptions interrupted by interruptions. After taking the two phone calls, you rush off to a luncheon. En route you return more calls from the car phone. Maybe your spouse is lonely—that's quite likely— but how can you possibly be?

The phrase "loneliness at the top" evokes the office of the chief executive of the United States: Abraham Lincoln, for example, alone at Soldiers' Home composing the Emancipation Proclamation; or Harry S Truman, deciding whether to drop the atomic bomb. There are times, especially during the crucible of crisis, when further advice and counsel cannot help. One person alone must make a decision. As Truman said, "If you've done the best you can—if you have done what you have to do—there is no use worrying about it. . . . You can't think about how it would be . . . if you had done another thing. You have to decide."

In periods of crisis, hard decisions are inevitably forced upward to the ultimate decision maker, the chief. I've had to make some tough decisions myself (no atomic bomb-level decisions, but tough enough for me). And as the new CEO, you'll have a few to make, too.

But managers at all levels experience pressure. Demands for results come from above, requests for resources from below. Attempts to influence decisions seem to arrive from every direction. Loneliness is not confined to the top, either. Especially when managers report to individuals with different values. When asked to do something they consider ethically questionable, managers experience a special sense of isolation. I can think of several times when there was no one to turn to but myself, long before I became a senior manager.

Women executives are even more subject to loneliness than men, especially as they gain altitude and enter the rarified, clubby male atmosphere at the top. Yet, even far below the "glass ceiling" they often experience the feeling of being shut out.

A survey by Catalyst, a New York-based nonprofit organization, found as recently as 1990 that nearly half of the human resources professionals surveyed (mostly men, of course) thought women had less initiative and took fewer risks than men. And if they took more initiative, and more risks, they then risked being rejected for those very "nonwomanly" traits.

Members of any minority group in the workplace must work hard to overcome a feeling of rejection or alienation, not to mention an even smaller minority group: pregnant managers. "Assume," says University of Georgia professor Dawn D. Bennett-Alexander, "that the perception is going to be that you are not the same productive, committed, aggressive worker you were before." Assume, too, that you may find yourself surrounded by people—even hearty well-wishers—but still feeling all alone by the telephone.

Loneliness seems to be a particular occupational hazard for the heads of colleges and universities. The objective of the job, one college president explained in a not so tongue-in-cheek manner, is to keep all of your constituencies (faculty, staff, students, trustees, benefactors, townspeople, athletic boosters, and so on) equally unhappy. In higher education, the consultation function has been institutionalized in such bodies as faculty senates, search committees, and student government associations. But the alienation of the university president is not just a recent phenomenon. William Rainey Harper, the first president of the University of Chicago, wrote this in 1904:

Another feeling which gradually grows upon the occu-
pant of the presidential chair is that of great loneliness
. . . the feeling of separation from all his fellows. At
certain times he realizes that in all truth he is alone; for
those who are ordinarily close to him seem to be, and
in fact, are, far away. . . . The college presidency means
the giving up of many things, and not the least among
them, one's most intimate friendships. Moreover, this
feeling of separation, of isolation, increases with each
recurring year, and, in spite of the most vigorous effort,
it comes to be a thing of permanence. This is inevitable,
and it is as sad as it is inevitable.

Father John Cavanaugh, who preceded Father Theodore M.
Hesburgh as president of the University of Notre Dame, described
one needed characteristic for the job as "personal courage, often
lonely courage, because everyone else below has passed the
buck." Without such courage, he said, "the presidency can be an
agony . . . a failure. Of that I am sure."

Dwelling in a fishbowl adds to the feeling of separation.

Harold W. Dodds, president of Princeton University from
1933 through 1957, made this observation: "Sooner or later a self-
examining president has moments when he wonders why he ever
took the job or what he is accomplishing that someone else could
not do better. He will suffer attacks of loneliness; he will be irri-
tated by days that slip completely away from his planned use of
them."

No Hiding Place

Like other chief executives, college presidents are subject to constant scrutiny. Dwelling in a fishbowl strangely adds to the feeling of separation. Former Yale University president (and later
commissioner of baseball) A. Bartlett Giamatti commented, "Not
that I've been treated unfairly, but you go from being a private

person to suddenly reading descriptions of your face, your clothes, the way your hands look."

At the top, the spotlight is *always* on you. Though AT&T's chairman Robert E. Allen is a great team player, there are times when he plays a solo role. An accomplished golfer, he describes his solitary business decision experience in golfing terms: "When you get down to making the shot, you're out there all by yourself, with the whole world to see."

One of Allen's predecessors at AT&T was Charles L. Brown, a shy and modest man (I once overheard his reply to someone who asked what he did: "I work for the telephone company") destined to face the most momentous decision in the history of AT&T. It must have been a lonely, wrenching moment in 1984 when he decided to recommend to his board that the company comply with, rather than appeal, Judge Harold Greene's ruling that AT&T be broken into pieces.

There are some chief executives—including some college presidents—who contribute to their isolation by their own behav-

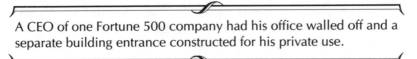

A CEO of one Fortune 500 company had his office walled off and a separate building entrance constructed for his private use.

ior. Benjamin Ide Wheeler, president of the University of California from 1899 to 1919, is reported to have ridden a white horse around campus, stopping from time to time to listen to the complaints of faculty members and students, then rendering his advice and announcing his decisions from horseback.

Some modern corporate chieftains, lacking this particular option, still manage to separate themselves by behavior that is seen by their people as equally bizarre. For example, a CEO of one Fortune 500 company, exhausted by constant questions from those around him, had his office walled off and a separate building entrance constructed for his private use.(All this while the company was financially hemorrhaging.)

But even effective leaders find exhaustion in their work, as well as isolation. Henry W. Wriston, president of Lawrence College and later of Brown University, and whose son Walter Wriston became chief executive of Citicorp, described his college presidencies this way:

> It is an arduous life. . . . Again and again at the end of
> the academic year, I was spent, physically and spiritu-
> ally. Hang on, get through commencement, then relax
> enough to recover energy and faith; that was the pre-
> scription. For thirty years it worked, sometimes by a
> narrow margin, at others by a wide one.

There are times when you simply *must* get away from the job.
Different people learn to do this in different ways. One CEO I
know (but only one) leaves the office each day early, short of a
genuine emergency. Another occasionally returns home from
business trips a day ahead of his published schedule. Still others
try to schedule a few hours of relaxation, or recreation, while on
business trips. As for myself, I've found an hour spent alone in a
nearby art museum to be highly therapeutic.

One of the ways CEOs differ is in their degree of outgoing-
ness. Dewitt Wallace, co-founder of *The Reader's Digest*, was pain-
fully shy and blanched at the prospect of having to give any kind
of speech. Some others are outgoing to a fault, choosing to surround themselves with people, in the manner of President
George Bush, at virtually every waking moment. Some are con-
templative, even reclusive.

One characteristic of successful leaders, however, is that they
are thinking creatures. They have the capacity to synthesize and
to conceptualize and the ability to sift through options. They
know how to make a solitary moment for themselves when necessary, despite the tumultuous pace of their activities. Such time
alone is essential for decision making and for self-definition. And
redefinition. The Chilean poet and diplomat Pablo Neruda has
written:

> All paths lead to the same goal: to convey to others what
> we are. And we must pass through solitude and diffi-
> culty, isolation and silence, in order to reach forth to the
> enchanted place where we can dance our clumsy dance
> and sing our sorrowful song.

Who Can I Trust?

To avoid clumsy decisions or sorrowful results, many managers
seek sounding boards, people they trust enough to confide in.

Such confidants can be helpful by posing questions that the manager may not have considered: What would be the effect of this on that, or what would happen if you were to defer a difficult decision, for example.

Finding reliable sounding boards within large organizations is generally not easy, and its difficulty increases in proportion to your responsibilities. The man or woman at the top has very limited options. If you select someone within the organization, you may be accused of playing politics. If you select an individual director, some member of the board with whom you feel comfortable, you will place that person in potential conflict because directors' loyalties (and legal responsibilities) are to the corporation, not to you. It's far better to choose an alter ego outside the company, a person whose trust and confidence has been richly earned. A good sounding board can help ease the estrangement of decision making, so it's well worth the effort to find one.

As president of The Conference Board, Kenneth Randall observed numerous chief executives. "Being a CEO is a lonely business," he said. "On this side of the desk there is no one else there with him. But on the other side it is excessively populated." Perhaps Kenneth Patchen's "Lonesome Boy Blues" says it best:

> *Oh lonesome's a bad place*
> *To get crowded into.*

Inevitably, men and women who arrive at the top find themselves surrounded by people and hemmed in by circumstance. Having now arrived there, you will need some private time to ponder important issues alone, and you'll need time for your family. But to be effective, most of the time you'll need to be fully engaged with others. Talking with your people. Calling on customers. Networking with your peers. Or stroking or schmoozing with your board.

Leadership requires active involvement. It cannot endure a retreat into yourself. Those who do retreat will suffer a self-inflicted estrangement that is ultimately crippling. It is only by leading your people in charge after charge, and *never* retreating into yourself, that you can avoid those lonesome CEO blues.

Chapter Seven

Delegation and Team Building: No Solo Acts, Please

Beethoven's *Fifth Symphony* was not the product of a task force. Cezanne did not ask a quality circle to refine his "Still Life with Apples." Though the authorship of Shakespeare's plays is questioned from time to time, no one has yet attributed them to a corporate committee.

There are many human endeavors that are best entrusted to single creative individuals—but getting things done through organizations is not among them. Instead, teamwork is needed, and so is delegation. Managers who act like the Lone Ranger should ask themselves how far he would have gotten without Tonto—and Silver!

If there is one skill that distinguishes leaders, it is their ability to delegate right. The most promising fast-track manager can get quickly derailed by delegating too much—or too little. An insecure first-line manager may fail to delegate through fear of failure. A general manager with an engineering degree may find it hard to let others make technical decisions. Chief executives who see themselves as marketing experts may second-guess their brand managers. Some CEOs, convinced they're utterly irreplaceable, are reluctant to retire (the act of ultimate delegation). How will their companies survive without them? (And, for that matter, vice versa?) Jeffrey Sonnenfeld, professor of management at Emory University, says the following:

It's very easy for them to believe in their own indispensability. They have made a difference, and without their companies they feel there is an abyss of insignificance. A violinist can do many things after leaving an orchestra, but a conductor only has the group.

Yet some active conductors still enjoy playing the violin. Or pounding the kettle drum.

Lee Iacocca, whose initials are often jokingly said to stand for "I Am Chairman Of Chrysler Corporation of America," was said in 1991 (at age 66) still to be dabbling in design. According to a recent news account:

Many Chrysler executives, engineers, and stylists complain that many of the company's car and truck models have sold poorly in recent years because of changes and delays ordered by Mr. Iacocca. The designers, in particular, roll their eyes when describing how Mr. Iacocca, with a wave of his cigar, has forced them to submit long, boxy designs and plenty of chrome, when rounder, cleaner models were clearly winning customers.

Whether or not you see Iacocca as a great CEO, his record was not achieved as a great delegator.

In contrast, PepsiCo's Wayne D. Calloway is seen by his people as a great delegator. Yet once asked whether the buzz word "empowerment" is a "silver bullet," he replied:

There are no silver bullets. But empowerment is important. You need that to feel, "This is my business and my company, and I am the steward of these assets." It's really important to us.

A recent internal study by PepsiCo found that one reason some of its managers failed was their overdeveloped egos. Calloway commented:

To be specific, the single biggest reason for failure at PepsiCo was arrogance. There is nothing wrong with confidence, but arrogance is something else. Arrogance is the illegitimate child of confidence and pride. Arrogance is the idea that not only can you never miss a duck, but no one else can ever hit one.

To become leaders, managers must abandon the attitude of "If I want anything done right I have to do it myself." The truth is that there are members of your team who can probably do many things better than you. Managers who fail to learn this lesson limit their ability to lead. Those who fail to delegate through fear of failure increase their probability of failure. Those who fail to delegate through arrogance will become humbled.

There are, however, some things you cannot delegate. Earlier, I discussed the CEO's special responsibility for the future. Delegating the planning function can put your career, and your company, at risk. And because the future is so heavily dependent upon your direct reports, you certainly cannot delegate their selection. You can call on executive search consultants to help find

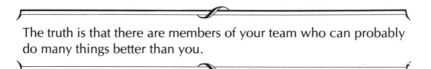

The truth is that there are members of your team who can probably do many things better than you.

candidates. Others can help screen out unsuitable ones. But in the end, you alone must choose.

Don G. Mitchell, former president of General Telephone and Electronics (GTE) Corporation and former chairman of General Time Corporation and Sylvania Electric Products, Inc., believes that there is only one "management fundamental" about staff selection: If a person is going to work directly for you, *you select that person*. Employees are not fungible commodities. Each comes with his or her own set of unique "management fingerprints": skills, attitudes, beliefs, values, and idiosyncrasies. Whether you will be able to delegate effectively to a particular person is a judgment you alone can make. Poor judgment in selection invites disaster. And the disaster will have *your* fingerprints all over it.

Remember: Delegation requires two parties and a relationship between those parties. Unless that relationship is based on trust, delegation cannot work. So, in selecting team members, you will want to keep these questions in mind: How confident will I be in delegating authority to this person? And how committed is he or she to the process of delegating to others?

At this point you may be saying, "Of course I will select my own direct reports. Why wouldn't I?" But the larger question is how committed are you to letting them select *their* direct reports? Will you let them make a mistake? How big a mistake will you let them make? And will their selection of the wrong people be *their* mistake, or yours? (Don't answer this question too quickly!)

Father Theodore M. Hesburgh, president of the University of Notre Dame for over three decades, had a prodigious work schedule both at the university and in public service. Fourteen presidential appointments involved him in such major social issues as civil rights, atomic energy, campus unrest, Vietnam amnesty, Third World development, immigration reforms, and conflict resolution. As Notre Dame's president he was remarkably accessible despite his packed calendar and fierce travel schedule. During his tenure there he developed strong ideas about how to delegate:

> You are an idiot if you think you can run a place this size and this complicated by yourself. What you have to do is sort it out into its component parts, which I tried to do with the vice-presidents, the deans, the department chairmen, and the directors of big functions on the nonacademic side. Then you try to find the very best people you can for these many assignments. *But I don't think that's my job.* What I tell each vice-president is this: "I want you to find the very best people you can find, but you are going to have to choose and appoint them, since you are going to work with the people you select. If they are successful, you're going to get the credit for the success of that operation, and if you pick the wrong people, who are unsuccessful, you are going to take the blame for it. I am not going to take the credit from you, and I am not going to take the blame for you."

If You Don't Understand It, Don't Delegate It

Delegation does not mean ignoring key aspects of your business, even areas outside your experience that may seem mysterious to you. Mastering the art of "managing the inscrutable" is a sine qua non for the person who wants to make it to the top. Very often, you can't simply leave engineering to the engineering vice-president or research to the scientist.

How much do you need to know? As CEO, you'd better know a lot, especially about the core of your business. When Louis V. Gerstner, Jr., left McKinsey to join American Express as executive vice-president of its TRS (Travel Related Services) Division, he already knew a lot about the core of its business, credit cards. At McKinsey, he had spent almost five years consulting with TRS. Yet when he landed at American Express, according to Harvard Business School professor John P. Kotter, he "shocked

> The trick is to delegate what you *do* understand, not what you *don't*.

the people running the card organization by bringing them together within a week of his appointment . . . and then proceeding to question all of the principles by which they conducted their business . . . and showed little tolerance for formal 'dog-and-pony' presentations."

The next year Gerstner became president of the TRS Division and later vice-chairman of American Express. Since 1989 he's been chairman and CEO of RJR Nabisco, and you can be sure that he now knows as much about the food and tobacco industry as anyone there. Gerstner's fact-digging and opinion-seeking activity on the way up in his career is typical of how the best CEOs operate, even the best delegators.

It is only by understanding the business that you *can* delegate with any confidence. The trick, of course, is to delegate what you *do* understand, not what you *don't*.

But the knowledge you may need to delegate confidently may extend far from your core business. In recent years, medical benefit costs have continued to escalate, and their containment has landed high on the agenda of most CEOs. In gatherings of chief executives this has been a common topic of discussion for many years. And I doubt you'd find any who are ignorant of the latest FASB rulings, no matter how arcane.

And it's not just knowledge about what you're managing that's essential. At this juncture it's very important to get to know your direct reports. In depth. If you've just taken over responsibility for a research group, for example, you'll need to assess your research director. What has he or she accomplished? Published? Made happen in your part of the company? Influenced in other parts of the company? Managed to get from the laboratory to the market? How is the research director regarded by the research staff?

Still, at this point it's *your* opinion that counts. Are you learning this new field quickly enough to manage it well? What help do you need? Calling on your predecessor would be useful, but what if he or she has gone to work for a competitor? Do the people in your new unit seem somehow strange? Perhaps you're now responsible for a few hundred research scientists. And your background is sales. Do they seem to be from a different planet? Or, coming from finance, with the sales manager now reporting to you, do the salespeople seem strangely gung ho? In either case, this is the time to put aside stereotypical thinking. I've found just as many prima donnas in sales as in research, in manufacturing as in public relations. Remember the old principle: Prima donnas are fine—as long as they can really sing.

"Why Did You Do That?"—A Sure Delegation Killer

Don Mitchell describes the two basic reasons that delegation fails: Either the person to whom you are delegating resists taking on the responsibility, or you may secretly want to keep that responsibility for yourself. Too often, it is the latter case.

Management is about accountability. Though you cannot delegate your personal accountability, you can make others accountable for their results. But only if you are willing to give them your authority—and live with their results.

This doesn't mean that every decision can be delegated. There are even times when you'll have to reverse your people's decisions. But such occasions should be rare. As Henry Kissinger says, "You've got no right to be CEO if you're not prepared to overrule your subordinates."

Arthur K. Watson, former CEO of the IBM World Trade Corporation, whimsically conveyed this thought in a rhetorical question: "What's the fun of being CEO if you can't make an arbitrary decision once in a while?" Still, your credibility as a leader will suffer in proportion to the frequency of such arbitrary decisions. A habit of reversing, or merely second-guessing your peoples' decisions, can destroy delegation throughout your organization. There are times when you'll just have to grit your teeth and smile. Remember, you're a role model. You need to back your people up, not back them down.

Entrepreneur Portia Isaacson believes in hiring people she can trust, and then trusting them. In speaking of scientists, she says the following:

> I somehow manage them without their knowing that they are being managed. . . . I tend to give direction from a distance, painting a broad picture on the wall and asking my people to go away and fill in the details. When they bring it back to me, I might say, "Well, I like all that—it's just wonderful—but this piece right here needs fixing." I never deal with details, yet I never fail to give direction.

Successful delegation requires judgment. How can you assess the judgment of your direct reports? When Yves Trellu was president and chief operating officer of Michelin Tire Corporation, he described an interesting approach. When you're on vacation, he said, you'll find you're occasionally called about some problem or another. Do your people interrupt your holiday to tell you about some less-than-earth-shattering event? Or do they fail to call when something really serious has happened? Too much of one or the other will tell you something about their judgment.

Still, this test may tell you something else. If several direct reports disappoint you by calling, or failing to call, inappropriately, this may suggest a lack not of judgment but of trust. And if they call erratically, maybe it's your inconsistency, not theirs, that is at fault. Maybe it's time to talk this over with your people.

Delegation cannot succeed without open communication. You need to know where things stand, and your people need to know where they stand. They need to tell you what you are doing or not doing to help them. And you need to listen in a nondefensive mood.

Team Wanted: Quarterbacks Need Not Apply

Listening to, and delegating to, your direct reports is an essential part of leadership. But you need more than direct reports. You need a team. And, as was discussed earlier, *you* need to pick the players and to remove those who cannot operate as part of the team.

In selecting your team members it is useful to observe how the best executive search consultants go about their work. Instead of joining a BOGSA (bunch of guys sitting around) to ask what-do-you-think-about-her-and-who-else-do-you-know kinds of questions, they start at the beginning. Long before searching their data bases for candidates, they spend time exploring the job

> For your team you'll need some players who don't have to be captains.

to be filled. What are the expectations of the person to whom the candidate will report? With whom will the candidate interact? What resources will be available? What will be the limits to the candidate's authority? Into what sort of culture will he or she be plunged? Under what circumstances did the previous incumbent leave?

The answers to these questions raise still other questions, each of which needs to be answered. It is only when this process is well under way that the headhunter even begins to hunt for heads.

Because it's your team you're recruiting, my advice is this: First, know thyself. Make a fresh inventory of your strengths and weaknesses. Look as objectively as possible at your management style and behavior. What skills do you lack? What are the characteristics of those you've worked best with in the past? After conducting this self-analysis you'll have a better idea of whom to look for. And you'll be in better shape to talk with candidates. Portia

Isaacson says she's learned enough about herself "to know that I am a great team player, so long as I am running the team." No doubt that's why she *is* an entrepreneur. But for your team you'll need some players who don't have to be captains.

A new manager seldom starts with a clean slate. Usually, some part of the team is already in place. So, having less than complete flexibility, you'll find it even more important to take stock of yourself. And you'll need to get to know in as much depth as possible the team members already on board. But whether or not you're starting with a tabula rasa, you'll want to surround yourself with the best people you can possibly find—people who, in their own fields, are better than you.

Because you are looking for a variety of team players, not a half-dozen quarterbacks, you'll want to think hard about their interpersonal skills. Even one serious turf protector can destroy a team's effectiveness. And yours.

Teamwork and Trust

After you've brought your players aboard, it's time to start building that team. Training programs can help, but there's no substitute for your own efforts.

Harvard Business School professor John J. Gabarro's research on managerial transitions emphasizes the importance of team building. The more successful managers, he found, were those most effective in building trust among their team members. Over time, members of your team will come to respect one another. Gradually, trust will develop. When you reach that point, you will have a team—not just a collection of people assigned to work with one another. And with a team you'll make better decisions than you ever could make on your own.

Although Robert Crandall, CEO of American Airlines, is a highly decisive person, he relies strongly on the opinions of his people. Every Monday morning he convenes a planning committee, made up of eight senior executives, which meets for long hours, often into the night. Crandall says, "I think you have to accept the notion that at the senior levels of any big company, you rarely know what the outcome of any decision is going to be. When we are making a decision, we do our best to elicit all the views about how the decision might come out. And we debate those views vigorously." During sessions such as these, something else is happening. Teams are being built.

Over the years meetings have developed a bad reputation. Most deserve it. Yet in team building there is no substitute for them. Your people need to meet with you in a group setting, time and again, before they can become an effective group. Disney CEO Michael Eisner describes the process: "You bring a bunch of disparate people in the room, you don't let them out, you don't feed them, you give them a sparse amount of water. And finally all of the inhibitions are gone and they are no longer trying to impress one another and they are no longer trying to impress you. And some really good ideas come out of it."

The importance of team building is not limited to the top echelons. First-line managers need to apply their highest standards in selecting team members and must give just as much attention to the team-building process. Indeed, because the first-line manager's team will be made up of men and women with little or no management experience, there is an even greater need for training. The work of managers at all levels has much in common, and it is a rare manager whose effectiveness cannot be improved through teamwork.

In 1989, Elliott Jaques published a seminal study on the nature of organization and management. Among other things he reported the discovery of what he calls time-span measurement. This measurement is based on the maximum target completion times of managers. A first-line manager, for example, may be expected to complete a particular project within six months, whereas his or her division general manager may be involved in a five-year effort to develop a new product and bring it to market. Further up the hierarchy there may be a group vice-president who is targeting some results scheduled ten years into the future. At the very top, according to Jaques, the CEO "must have at least a 25-year perspective-setting strategic outreach if the corporation is to be expected to survive in the long term."

The correlation between time span and organizational level was confirmed in studies of over one hundred organizations. Jaques's finding has application to a number of issues, including management compensation and span of control. He points out, for example, that contrary to the conventional wisdom that no more than five or six people should report to one manager, it is circumstances that determine span of control. Depending on those circumstances, a manager can deal with between one and seventy immediate direct reports while maintaining the necessary knowledge and relationships required to get the job done.

But as one moves upward in an organization, complexity increases along with targeted time spans. And as complexity grows, so does the level of abstraction. Those at the working level deal directly with machines, perhaps, or with customers, whereas those at the top are coping with numbers, concepts, and models of reality—instead of reality itself. For this reason, the teams at the top must constantly seek out and confront reality.

Whether at the top or elsewhere, teams vary in size, composition, purpose—and effectiveness. Usually, the more diverse its members, the more effective the team. So whenever you're putting one together, seek out men and women from different levels within your organization, managers with differing time-span perspectives and people of different ages, attitudes, and assumptions, if you hope to draw upon the power of teamwork at its best.

Teams at the Top?

At lower levels, job sharing represents one kind of team endeavor. But in some companies even the topmost positions are held by more than one person. Nordstrom, Inc., the retail chain, provides an extreme example. There the title of chairman is shared by four members of the founding Nordstrom family. In May 1991, four nonfamily members of management were named to the new post of co-president. Though this case of eight individuals sharing the two top offices is quite rare, it is not unusual for companies to establish an office of the chairman, or president, consisting of two or more people. In 1992, for example, Microsoft created a three-person office of the president, and Xerox, a six-member "corporate office" designed to operate in place of a president. But even in the traditional one-person, one-title structure, none of these top jobs can actually be accomplished by one man or woman alone. Still, one strong leader can—and must—serve as the catalyst for a nucleus of a team.

The history of business is replete with examples of two-man

,teams at the top. The impulsiveness of IBM's chairman Thomas J. Watson, Jr., was for years balanced by the studied calm of its president Albert L. Williams. In his autobiography, Watson wrote:

> In spite of the mistakes we made, I couldn't have run IBM without Al. He was my alter ego. He had the ability to be analytical while I was intuitive and to make sure everything was tightened up and done right while I was out in front setting the pace for the business. Without him my success would not have been possible.

Honda Motor Company, Ltd., would not have achieved its global presence had the brilliant inventor Soichiro Honda not teamed up with Takeo Fujisawa, who provided the financial and organizational expertise. When Walt Disney Co. needed new leadership in 1984, Michael Eisner of Paramount Pictures and Frank Wells of Warner Bros., Inc., joined Disney as a team. (Eisner is chairman and CEO, and Wells is president and COO.) At Coca-Cola Co. the long-running team of chairman and CEO Roberto Goizueta and president and COO Donald Keough has had great success. At Capitol Cities/ABC, Inc., the formidable Tom Murphy/ Dan Burke team represents leadership at its best.

New "two-man" leadership teams are being formed every day across every industry. In 1991, Fox, Inc., chairman Barry Diller hired Lucie Salhany away from Paramount to become chairman of Fox's Twentieth-Century television unit. She and Diller, who is known to be highly demanding, would face that industry's intense competition together. "I like that challenge," she said. "I'm at my very worst when things are going well." (However, only a half-year later, Diller—barely age 50—resigned to strike out on his own.)

Of course, not all teams at the top succeed. C. Fred Fetterolf, former president of Aluminum Co. of America, had teamed up wonderfully with chairman Charles A. Parry. But a few years after Paul O'Neill succeeded Parry as Alcoa's CEO, Fetterolf resigned, citing differences with O'Neill on "important business principles."

Top teams that are created through mergers face a special challenge. In early 1992, for example, Time Warner's co-chief executive N. J. Nicholas, Jr. (formerly of Time), received a director's phone call at his Vail, Colorado, condo telling him he would be replaced, on the very next day, by Vice-Chairman Gerald M. Levin. Levin would immediately join Steven J. Ross (former Warner CEO) as new co-chief of Time Warner. Nothing personal, of course.

Still, when these management pairings at the top do work, some seem almost magical.

But even if magic does enter into some of these happy partnerships, you'd better not count on it. Instead, just do what has to be done, step by step, to build your team. Most important, build trust. I'm sure you'll find, as I have, that trust is the secret ingredient of every successful team. And it's one of those things that you can gain only by generously giving it. Through trust, authority can be successfully dispersed rather than hoarded at the top. The CEO can then do his or her job with assurance that others will do theirs.

How Many Hats Can a CEO Wear?

Some senior executives hold multiple jobs. In July 1991, *The New York Times* reported that David B. Mathis, then president and COO of the Kemper Corporation, would be named chairman and CEO, but would retain his current title as well. About a week later the *Times* reported that Harvey Golub, American Express's vice-chairman and chairman of its subsidiary, IDS Financial Services, had been given the additional title of president of American Express and would join its chairman and CEO, James D. Robinson 3rd, in a newly created "office of the chairman." (Are you still with me?) Only a few months later, Golub added two *more* titles: Chairman and CEO of American Express's TRS Division.

Multiple-title holders like Mathis and Golub are not rarities. Business writer Anthony J. Michels estimates that 15 percent of those who head Fortune 500 companies hold *all three* of the top jobs of president, chairman, and chief executive. Donald C. Hambrick, a professor at Columbia University's Graduate School of Business, calls this the "Idi Amin phenomenon," alluding to the tendency of the former Ugandan president to confer title after title upon himself. But Brunswick Corporation's chairman, president, and CEO Jack S. Reichert claims that in highly decentralized organizations in which strong divisional presidents report directly to the CEO, this kind of arrangement makes sense. Still, when one person holds many operating responsibilities, where does he or she find time to manage the future? Or to go to the washroom?

A Delegator for All Seasons

Skill in delegation develops only over time. And the way you practice it can change markedly the longer you are in an assignment. A new first-line manager, by definition, has no experience in delegating responsibility to direct reports. The general manager has to learn delegation on the way up. To successful CEOs, delegation becomes second nature. But in each new assignment there is a tendency to keep team members on a short leash. The longer managers are in their assignments, the more they tend to delegate. This is especially true of chief executives.

Robert W. Lear, executive-in-residence at Columbia University's Graduate School of Business and former CEO of F. & M. Schaefer, believes there are three stages or "passages" in a chief executive's tenure, each lasting two to five years. In the first stage the CEO takes the "boldest steps to change the business and its overall direction." In the second stage the CEO discovers the outside world (and hops around it in the company plane) but still spends time—though less time—on operations. The third and final stage is characterized by the CEO's attempting to refine the company's vision but also devoting more and more time to outside activities. At this stage, Lear says, "CEOs still are in charge of the company, but not in the way they used to be." He recommends that by the time the chief begins the passage into the third stage, the board should select a new CEO and designate the current one as chairman. (The Catch-22, of course, is that by this time, the CEO probably has the board firmly in his or her pocket.)

Research by Professor Donald C. Hambrick at Columbia University suggests that the largest contributor to continued change may be the capacity and diversity of the CEO's top team and "his willingness to listen to that team for fresh, divergent insights." The chief executive, to delegate successfully, must forge a strong top team. Paradoxically, its members gain their strength only by being given increasingly larger responsibilities and authority. Yet to be given these responsibilities they must have the CEO's confidence.

It is clear that the process of delegation must begin by a spark of faith. Kindled by accomplishment, it is ultimately sustained by trust. Effective delegators are the managers (at *all* levels) who believe in their people as much as in themselves and who know that from that belief comes not just accomplishment, but growth.

Chapter Eight

Making Time: The Impossible Dream?

The crucial shortage of time at the executive level is hardly a recent phenomenon. "Go, Sir, gallop, and don't forget that the world was made in six days," wrote Napoleon Bonaparte to one of his aides. "You can ask me for anything you like," he continued, "except time."

You and I have access to a vast array of time-saving devices, but our discretionary time is as limited as Napoleon's. The cellular telephone lets you leave the office even when expecting an important call. With voice mail there's no need to play telephone tag. Express-mail services let you return from a long business trip to a clean desk. And the fax machine has been absorbed into the American culture. In Manhattan, I recently spotted this T-shirt message: "You never fax me anymore." By now there may even be country music bewailing the unfaxed lover.

With the increased pace of American business, we need all the help we can get. But we often seem to use modern office technology for the same reason that Sir Edmund Hillary climbed Mount Everest: because it's there. Surely not every fed-exed or faxed document requires such urgent transmission. But too busy to think, we find ourselves unable to distinguish between the urgent and the merely important. Lest you believe you are immune to this, find out how many faxes are sent from your office each month. Also, when you're personally sending a fax message (because you're too impatient to wait for your assistant to do it), have you ever found yourself cursing the machine for operating too *slowly*? Maybe it's time for you to take a break and to reflect on just where all your time goes.

About forty years ago, a study was made in Sweden to find out what business executives actually did and how their time was spent. Professor Sune Carlson and his associates, following twelve Swedish chief executives around with stopwatches, learned that their workdays were made up of hundreds of small blocks of time. Indeed, none of them enjoyed more than twenty uninterrupted minutes during the entire study. (Why doesn't this surprise us?)

Some years later, Henry Mintzberg, now a professor at McGill University, studied the question of how managers actually manage. Synthesizing the findings of observations made in North America and Europe, Mintzberg exploded a number of myths about the job of the manager. Forget planning and control. He described the work pace for both CEOs and foremen as unrelenting. "The chief executives met a steady stream of callers and mail from the moment they arrived in the morning until they left in the evening. Coffee breaks and lunches were inevitably work related, and ever-present subordinates seemed to usurp any free moment." Half of the activities of the CEOs studied by Mintzberg lasted less than nine minutes, and only 10 percent took more than an hour.

The fragmented nature of managers' time was not limited, however, to chief executives. It existed at every level. Delving into the reasons for this, Mintzberg analyzed the nature of management and identified ten separate roles that managers must fill. Like a one-person Broadway show with the star playing ten parts (rushing off stage between scenes for costume changes), the modern manager is severely pressed. But this is only one aspect of the picture, for the many associates the manager is interacting with in each of his or her roles are all playing their own multiple roles.

Professor Leonard A. Sayles of Columbia University compares the role of a manager to that of a symphony orchestra conductor who is:

> endeavoring to maintain a melodious performance in which the contributions of the various instruments are coordinated and sequenced, patterned and paced, while the orchestra members are having various per-

sonal difficulties, stagehands are moving music stands
. . . and the sponsor of the concert is insisting on irra-
tional changes in the program.

Add to this the complication that the manager is more than a conductor. At times he or she must perform a solo part. Or abandon
the orchestra to write up an important report. Or leave the concert
hall completely to call on customers. Or deal with crises. Is it any
wonder then that there's a shortage of time?

The New Time Crunchers Take Their Toll

Developments in recent years have created an even greater time
gap. Downsizing, now a way of life, has stripped away many of
the support services that we once enjoyed. Spans of control have
increased. Managers have been forced to take on additional responsibilities, new and unfamiliar. As we climb steep learning
curves, attempting to master unfamiliar tasks while juggling our
regular work loads, time becomes even scarcer. Sociological
trends have also taken their toll. When both husbands and wives
work outside the home, there is less time available to tend to
everyday chores. Something has got to give. What is usually sac-
rificed is an hour or two of needed sleep. So we return to the
workplace less rested than we were the night before, to tackle an
increasingly complex work load. Then we head home at the end
of the day wondering where all the time went.

According to the University of Maryland's John P. Robinson,
who directs its Americans' Use of Time Project, "a large segment
of Americans say they feel a significant crunch—and the more
time needy they feel, the stronger their desire to take time off."
In a recent study, Robinson found that 50 percent of over a thou-
sand people polled said they'd be willing to trade a full day's pay
for an extra day off each week.

Increasingly, time pressures are making managers question
their values. Just how satisfying is a high-paying job if there is no
time to enjoy its rewards? Parents in the workplace are the most
pressed of all—pressed by time and pressed by guilt. One woman
puts it this way:

> Every morning, [when] my son watches me get dressed
> . . . he says, "No work, Mama. Stay home. Play here."
> Then after I take him to the babysitter, I get to drive
> away waving to my little crying boy in the window. Nice
> start on the day, huh? It makes me crazy.

She goes on to say that both parenthood and work are diminished and that satisfaction is diluted in both arenas.

Then there are the many men and women who find themselves in management jobs they just can't master, victims of the Peter Principle. Given sufficient time, they might succeed. As for the rest of us, given *inadequate* time, we might fail. Where does the time go? Can we find a way to cope?

Where the Time Flies (Even When You're Not Having Fun)

One person who has studied these questions for over twenty years is Alec MacKenzie. He has met with managers at hundreds of companies around the world and concluded that the reasons for time scarcity are remarkably similar across management levels, industries, and national borders. The five biggest time wasters, he claims, are these:

1. Management by crisis
2. Telephone interruptions
3. Inadequate planning
4. Attempting too much
5. Drop-in visitors

But there are many more: the inability to delegate; not knowing how to say no; procrastination. The list goes on.

As MacKenzie points out, management by crisis means dealing with a crisis *after* it occurs, rather than preventing it from happening. I completely agree. Some years ago a commercial airline pilot was highly praised for his calm in the face of a severe emergency. After a long, upside-down free fall, he managed to right his aircraft and save the lives of everyone aboard. Not long after that, however, the pilot was fired; an investigation showed it was his error that caused the plane to drop from the sky in the first place.

Crises in business, as elsewhere, are often self-inflicted. All around us are accidents waiting to happen. When they occur, time management goes out the window. Advice given by a retiring president of a small southern university to his successor included this: Don't let your schedule get so packed that you have no time for disaster. In almost every academic year during his tenure, some unforeseen crisis had arrived. Sure enough, shortly after the new president took office, several undergraduate student leaders were killed and others critically injured in an unavoidable automobile accident. Working with the students' parents and friends took immediate priority over every scheduled activity for many days. When Johnson & Johnson's Tylenol packages were injected with cyanide in the 1980s, its chairman and CEO James Burke's schedule went out the window. The aftermath of the poisonous gas leakage in Bhopal, India, in 1984 con-

> Don't let your schedule get so packed that you have no time for disaster.

sumed every waking hour of Union Carbide's top management team for months. Obviously not all crises are avoidable, but many are. More important, the fact that there *will* be crises must be recognized. All managers should be clear about who will be given the authority to act for them in times of extreme emergency.

In today's lean organizations, the loss of a single key person may in itself create a crisis. So it's vital that you decide ahead of time just who has the strength to take on more responsibility. And don't allow yourself to be so tightly scheduled that emergencies can't be taken in stride. If you do, then little crises will become big ones, and big crises will simply be unmanageable.

MacKenzie's second most frequent time waster is the telephone. He suggests that whenever possible you have someone take your calls, screening out the unimportant ones. My experience suggests otherwise. I prefer to answer my own calls (unless, of course, I'm in a meeting). To me the value of being immediately accessible to customers and employees far outweighs the benefit of the small amount of time saved. And I value the time of my administrative assistant. The nature of her job is more stressful than mine—inasmuch as I have more control over my schedule than she has over hers. Also, interruptions to her work will inter-fere with important jobs she's doing for me.

The third and fourth most popular time wasters are interre-lated: inadequate planning and attempting to do too much. We can avoid the latter by doing a better job of planning and also by simply learning to say no. As a manager rises in any organization, demands for his or her time increase. Your assistant can help to protect you from unproductive meetings and other time-wasting activities, but it's you who must learn to manage your own hours and minutes.

Finally, there is the drop-in visitor. Old Charley, who retired five years ago, is in town and just thought he'd drop by to talk (and talk and talk and talk) over old times or maybe give you some advice. You don't want to be discourteous, but there is a company to run. After a respectable few minutes, during which he should have your undivided attention, you might stand and thank him for the visit, explaining that you have a meeting to attend. Better still, walk with him to the lobby (or to someone else's office, if all else fails) and say goodbye there. If you don't learn how to handle this involuntary exit procedure gracefully, Old Charley will put you on his regular visitation rounds.

Time-Savers That Work

Despite the best advice available from time-management experts, managers must determine for themselves how best to manage their time. Just as important as reducing your time-wasting activ-ities is identifying personal time-*saving* techniques. Among those I've found useful are these:

• *Learn to listen.* By concentrating on one topic at a time, set-ting aside any distracting thoughts, you can shorten the length of meetings. This is especially true in negotiations. An approach I learned from an executive I worked closely with for many years is this: First, let the other person present his or her position fully and thoroughly. Let him do all the talking. Listen so intently that after his point of view has been expressed, you play it back. Repeat exactly what you've heard. By doing this, you'll show that you completely understand his point of view. And on hearing you play it back, he will almost always moderate his position—even before you've presented yours. Besides, you've set an example and encouraged him to listen to *your* position.

• *Master delegation.* Take time especially to develop a good working relationship with your assistant, a person whom Jim Martin, former chairman of Massachusetts Mutual Life Insurance Company, calls an "unsung hero." This is the first place to start with team building. And remember: Effective delegation comes through consistency of behavior. If your actions are unpredictable, your people will be afraid to take responsibility for fear of being second-guessed. Finally, always ask yourself what added value you can *personally* bring to a task. If someone else can provide greater added value than you, then immediately delegate it.

• *Use common sense.* For example, if you want to avoid playing telephone tag with a CEO of another company, place your call very early in the morning or very late in the day. That's the most likely time to find the CEO alone in his or her office with no one else to answer the call. Take time to think about the relative importance of your activities. Tackle the important ones at the time of day when you're least pressed by others' demands. To keep unscheduled meetings brief, walk over to the office of the person you need to talk to. By doing so, you can leave as soon as you've accomplished your purpose.

• *Handle routine matters as they come up.* My habit is to return calls as promptly as possible, rather than let them pile up. If you get back quickly, the caller is likely to still be near the telephone, with the matter at hand still fresh in mind. Routine decisions of a simple nature should be made quickly in order to get minor distractions behind you. Try to keep your mind clear.

• *Maintain calendar integrity.* If you make a commitment, keep it. This will help to build trust and save time in the long run. Just as important, think about what you're about to commit *to*. A one-hour speech will take many hours to prepare, for example. Are you giving that speech for the good of the business? Or just to feed your ego? And who controls your calendar? You and your assistant can't *both* do it without one or the other of you making an error.

• *Take charge.* Only by being proactive and purposeful, only by focusing on results, can your time be best spent. This is the greatest time-saver of all.

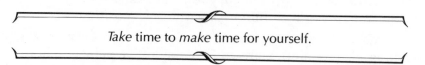

Take time to *make* time for yourself.

Schedule time for yourself. Jack Welch, chairman and CEO of General Electric, has one of the most demanding jobs in the world. But he says, "If someone tells me, 'I'm working 90 hours a week,' I'd say, 'You're doing something terribly wrong. I go skiing on the weekend. I go out with my buddies on Friday and party. You've got to do the same or you've got a bad deal. Put down a list of the things you're doing that make you work 90 hours, and ten of them have to be nonsense, or else somebody else has got to do them for you.' " So cut out the nonsense. And *take* time to *make* time for yourself.

Chapter Nine

Ambition and Greed,
or How to Lose by Winning

Winning isn't everything, it's the only thing.

Show me a good loser and I'll show you a loser.

We are NUMBER ONE!

Sound familiar? Whatever your corporate rallying cry, chances are it would apply just as well to any contact sport. Maybe better. Indeed, business language contains many sports allusions. The home run. Touching base. Acing it. Out of bounds. The end run. The touchdown. The goal.

The goal, of course, is for your team to win. And for that you'll need team spirit. Sadly, however, these aggressive slogans apply to many individuals who are not team players. Instead, they somehow need to see *themselves* as number one. Their ambition is to win, all right, but to win by being the star. If the team loses, that's someone else's fault. What matters is the star's number of points, not the team's.

Some managers are driven by an overwhelming need to achieve. Or a need for power. Or recognition. In short, they're driven by ambition. Symptoms of overambitious managers are usually very clear. They take full credit for their team's achievements and for others' ideas as well. They hoard information to themselves and create their own fiefdoms. Their actions destroy teamwork within their own work units and between their units and others. Still, by seeming to be on top of their jobs at all times, and by deft politics, they may rise high in the organization. Some even make it to the top. When they do, nothing is ever enough for the overambitious CEO. Not enough compensation, not enough perks. Not enough plaques and scrolls. Today, we even hear the term "trophy wives," used to describe some CEOs' glamorous second wives who replaced first wives who were not adequately glitzy.

For managers who hold important responsibilities, and certainly for CEOs, a well-developed ego is useful, perhaps even essential. You've got to have enormous self-confidence and self-esteem to do the tough jobs that must be done. To make decisions affecting thousands of people's lives. To lead your company in a totally new direction. To bet its assets, or much of them, on a new, untested product strategy. It takes a healthy ego, too, to stand before your shareholders, explaining last year's poor results and promising better. Or to carry your end of the conversation with an important political figure.

But surrounded by admirers and cushioned by luxurious trappings, many chief executives not only like the taste of success (however they measure it) but develop an appetite for more. Some want to pamper themselves. Others need to prove themselves.

In his book, *American Dreams*, Studs Terkel recorded dozens of verbatim interviews with a variety of people. Some talked about their ambition. Ted Turner, founder of the Turner Broadcasting System, creator of CNN, winner of the America's Cup, president of the Atlanta Braves, and chairman of the Atlanta Hawks, said this:

> I always wanted to win. I didn't win at that many things. I eventually found sailing and business. It's not the actual winning. . . . It's *trying* to win. . . . When I lay my baseball bat in the rack for the final game, I'd like to have people look back and just gasp at what I did in my lifetime.

Turner has had remarkable success. His talents and risk-taking capability seem to have yielded the results his ambitions demanded. In 1992, long before his final game, he was named by *Time* magazine as "Man of the Year," and he and his bride, Jane Fonda, were named "Couple of the Year" by *Newsweek*.

Wallace Rasmussen, former chief executive officer of Beatrice Foods, said:

> Years ago, I took my wife to Tulsa. I was ready to get on the airplane when the fellow said: "Don't you have your wife with you?" I said: "Oh, my gosh, yes." I forgot her [*laughs*]. People would say they saw me on the street and I didn't say hello. . . . It isn't my nature to be friendly. Whenever you're going to work for somebody, make sure you make him successful. Otherwise, you must jump over him.

Jumping over people is one way to succeed. But overambitious managers just walk over them.

Jumping over people is one way to succeed. But overambitious managers just walk over them. Others in the organization simply become mechanisms to help such managers reach their goals.

Hubris in High Places

When vanity and ambition combine, hubris is the inevitable result. Former Salomon Brothers chairman John Gutfreund transformed the once dignified brokerage firm into a bond-trading casino with an *Animal House* culture. Chronicled by Michael Lewis in *Liar's Poker*, caricatured in Tom Wolfe's *The Bonfire of the Vanities*, Gutfreund continued to be too ambitious by half. In 1991, he and Salomon Brothers president Thomas Strauss resigned (as did their general counsel and law *firm!*) as a result of alleged manipulation of the United States Treasury bond market. Among other things, it was reported that one Salomon managing director and a customer had conspired to play a "practical joke" on a bond salesman through a fraudulent $1 billion Treasury note "buy" order. Boys will be boys.

A few years earlier, in 1988, former boy wonder F. Ross John-

son, then CEO of RJR Nabisco, attempted without success a lev-
eraged buyout that landed him on the cover of a national news
magazine as a symbol of corporate greed. And out of the company.

In 1991, the nation watched as Clark Clifford, the courtly old-
hand counsellor to four U.S. presidents, tried to explain his role
as chairman of the First American Bank. This *éminence grise*,
whose autobiography celebrated his unwavering prudence and
wisdom, had a hard time persuading congressmen that he somehow never knew that the bank he chaired was owned by B.C.C.I.
(popularly known as the Bank of Criminals and Crooks International), which, not so incidentally, he had once served as legal
counsel. Apparently careful all his life to avoid conflicts of interest, he was unable to recognize any conflict in those relationships,
as was his young protégé, First American Bank president Robert
Altman. Both had borrowed heavily from B.C.C.I. to purchase
First American stock, and eighteen months later made a profit of
almost $10 million on the sale of the stock.

In a speech to a group of lawyers, while investigations were
still underway, Clifford quoted Horace Greeley: "Fame is a vapor;
popularity an accident; riches take wing. Those who can cheer
today, may curse tomorrow. Only one thing endures: character."
Some in the audience must have wondered about that.

There are many less dramatic examples of hubris at the top.
In recent years, CEO compensation has reached hubristic peaks,
even during recessionary periods. According to *Business Week*, in
1988 Disney's Michael Eisner made $40 million. In 1989, Craig
McCaw, of McCaw Cellular Communications, made almost $54
million. The winner the next year? Possibly Time Warner's Steven
J. Ross, at $78 million. Then there was LIN Broadcasting's Donald
A. Pels, whose payout after his company was acquired by McCaw
was $186 million. And, as this book went to press, the earnings
champion for 1991 appeared to be Coca-Cola's Roberto C. Goizueta—at a cool $86 million, which included a stock bonus of one
million shares. (At his 1992 annual meeting, he reminded shareholders that Coke's stock price had increased fourteenfold during
his tenure; still, some observers wondered whether *any* record of
accomplishment could justify a level of compensation exceeding
$1.6 million per *week*.)

Published figures like these, some CEOs complain, don't

take into account that their rewards may have been earned over a period of several years—through stock options, for example. But, it should be added, neither do these figures include commitments, in many cases, for staggering future payouts in the form of stock options or deferred compensation. Then there is the golden parachute, rightfully named. Multimillion-dollar parachutes are no longer uncommon. And they're triggered by a "change of control," for which read a *loss* of control by the CEO.

And now, even as many observers are expressing their outrage over excessive executive compensation, there's something new: the "golden coffin." Steven J. Ross, for example, who is hardly destitute (having been among the top Gold Cup winners of all time), will receive his base salary and "performance" bonus for three years after his death (as will about 15 percent of other Fortune 500 CEOs). Some are already "enjoying" this benefit. Armand Hammer, who died with his Occidental Petroleum boots on, is drawing down $2.3 million annually and will continue to receive this amount (though it's far from clear how to reach him) until 1998. Who said you can't take it with you?

Greed and More Greed

Soaring CEO pay is justified by compensation consultants (who in turn are paid by the CEO or the board—and I haven't even touched on the curious excesses of board compensation) as the need to keep the competition away. But A. F. Kaulakis of Chatham, New Jersey, asked an interesting question in a 1991 letter to *Business Week*: "Who would try to hire away John Akers of IBM or Lawrence Rawl of Exxon or Rand Araskog of ITT [anyway]?" His answer: "No one."

But all this, and very substantial benefits too, is not enough for some. In 1990, Lee Iacocca (who in 1989 had been rated by *Business Week* for the third straight year as the CEO who'd earned shareholders the least amount for his pay) received *only* a 15 per-

Now there's something new: the "golden coffin."

cent raise. Yet Chrysler's earnings were heading south. Perhaps to mollify him, the Chrysler board disclosed in its proxy statement (as it was a legal requirement to do so) that Chrysler was purchasing his two houses, one in Bloomfield, Michigan, and the other in Boca Raton, Florida. With his new wife, Iacocca had moved to a condominium north of Detroit. A Chrysler spokesman gave this explanation: "We treated him as if he was moving away and was being transferred to do this job." Just like any other employee. But what job? Did I miss something about a new job?

Most such special handling is perfectly legal, of course, but some comes close to crossing the line. In 1985, Allegheny International's CEO Robert J. Buckley wanted a house. And his board hadn't bought him one. His directors had given him (and some of themselves) almost everything else. But no house. So, a dummy corporation set up by Allegheny simply bought him one—a magnificent English Tudor home in a posh Pittsburgh neighborhood. And they furnished it for an amount somewhat less than its purchase price. Shortly after *Business Week* carried an extraordinary cover story based on its own investigation (not the board's investigation, not the SEC's investigation), Buckley decided to retire. Meanwhile, his son had been managing (with minimal qualifications, it was reported) a Manhattan hotel that had been purchased by Allegheny International. And there were other irregularities as well.

Some chief executives simply hold themselves above the ethical tenets that must be adhered to by mere mortals. Some, like Buckley, have put corporate assets to their personal use, going far beyond the bounds of appropriate executive perks. Some seem not only unencumbered by conscience but devoid of common sense, blinded by overindulged appetites—for luxury, ostentation, fame, or power. Some (but too few) have been toppled by their boards of directors. But ultimately by their own greed or ambition.

Unharnessed ambition at the top can lead to failure with dishonor or, as in the case of Michael Milken, formerly chief junk-bond trader at Drexel Burnham Lambert, to jail. And don't forget E. F. Glutton, er, Hutton. Destroyed by mismanagement, guilty by admission of 2,000 counts of fraud, this once prestigious brokerage firm sold its sorry remains to Shearson Lehman. Even *after* this sale, Hutton's directors awarded themselves more than $2.5

million in retirement benefits—just before turning out the light. Its CEO, Robert Fomon, had negotiated an $11 million "golden handshake." Still, he would miss the beautiful Hutton women (or, as he called them, "girls") he had reportedly bedded, not to mention the convenience. According to a Fomon confidant, "he considered it the spoils of war." And, in his early 60s, he still *liked* girls. "They're decorative, nice to look at, and have keen senses of humor," he told a fashion magazine editor. And no doubt they helped take his mind away from the business. Or *something* did.

Trapped by Success

At lower levels of the management structure, overambition can lead to great frustration. Stymied and stuck, their ambitions unfulfilled, such managers can feel trapped, emotionally wounded, despairing. Eventually they confront their dilemmas and temper their ambitions with reality, or they break. In contrast, the successes of some managers outrace their ambitions. Either way, something has to give.

Amy Saltzman, author of *Down-Shifting*, spoke with many managers who, after undergoing career crises, reflected on their experiences.

> Many conceded that even as their achievements on the job were pushing them into areas they didn't want to be, they felt compelled to put in longer hours and work harder for the next promotion. The result was that the more successful they became, the further they drifted from the kind of lives they really wanted to lead.

Some felt they had to accept promotions they did not really want. Richard Pinto, vice-president for operations for Marriott Residents Inns at the time, said he "just felt [he] was in a position where it would have been impossible to say no. . . . It just seemed to be inexorable the way things were going."

Edith Gilson, former senior vice-president of J. Walter Thompson, had had too many years of fourteen-hour days. "I worked so hard to get where I was, I couldn't imagine just pulling back," she said. "I felt I needed to make a total break." To get away from her stressful life, she moved from the New York area to the Berkshires, where she met dozens of other corporate dropouts. Like her, many had failed to fully understand the practical consequences of simply walking away from their jobs. Said Gilson: "They gave up their lives and their careers and ended up experiencing a real sense of loss." No wonder that stressed-out managers feel trapped. The romantic concept of saying "Take this job and shove it" is outweighed by the shock of the real. Gilson's chilling explanation: "This isn't a movie role. It's real life."

But work is real life, too. And even if you are not overambitious, your manager may be. If your chief executive is driving the organization to set some sort of record just to fulfill his or her quirky psychic needs, you may be caught up in the aftermath of a naked ego.

What can be done when your or others' ambition has made your work life unbearable? Dropping out of the rat race is one way out. But heading for the Berkshires is not a realistic option for most people. Still, finding a suitable job whose compensation matches your current one can be difficult or impossible. Managers trapped this way may feel that leaving is simply not feasible. Hoping beyond hope for some change—for example, a transfer to some other job in the company—they keep grinding on. "*Hope* is the thing with feathers," said Emily Dickinson, "That perches in the soul/And sings the tune without the words/And never stops—at all."

But under conditions utterly beyond your control, that feathered thing may fly away or die. Despair takes over. Sleepless nights are followed by bone-grinding, mind-numbing days. Your sense of humor no longer lubricates relationships. Depression sets in. Anyone who has experienced a serious depression knows the damage it can wield to your effectiveness, during this dark night of your soul. And that night is dark indeed if, upon reflection, you recognize that it was your own overambition that led you to that night.

These words of Yeats could apply to managers whose charred psyches led to their fall from the career ladder:

> Now that my ladder's gone,
> I must lie down where all the ladders start,
> In the foul rag-and-bone shop of the heart.

Is It Worth the Price?

Extreme emotional depression is quite common in the workplace. In March 1991, Rick Chollet, founder of Brookstone, an enormously successful retailer of household tools, took his life. For a long time, his wife said, Chollet had "swung from feeling totally powerful to totally helpless." Every chief executive has these conflicting feelings from time to time. When Chollet's suicide was described on a morning television show in Boston, a woman viewer called in to say that she, too, had recently attempted to take her life because of the pressures of running her successful business and feared she might try it again. "It's just so overwhelming," she said. "Everyone looks at me as a leader and all I want to do is run."

Washington psychoanalyst Douglas LaDier believes that half the *successful* work force is depressed. (Think of those who are *not* successful.) Psychotherapist Steven Berglas has a name for the executive success syndrome: "encore anxiety"—the fear of not being able to surpass or even match earlier accomplishments.

In Japan, suicide is seldom practiced by successful executives. There the tradition of hara-kiri is reserved for those who have failed and been publicly humiliated. But in recent years, a number of Japanese executives have died as a result of encore anxiety and stress in that demanding, achievement-driven society. While this is not a frequent occurrence, it has happened often enough that the Japanese have coined a word for it, *karoshi*.

I was a friend of one such Tokyo executive and observed his high-charging, driven behavior. Just before he died of a heart attack at a sports event his company was hosting, he was seen furtively making business calls on a hand-held phone while awkwardly trying to applaud—phone in hand.

Before such crises occur, there are usually warning signs, though often they are obscured by psychic blinders. Richard O. Jacobs, a Florida attorney who took a leave of absence from his law practice to become CEO of a failing bank, describes his experience in *Crashlanding: Surviving a Business Crisis*. On the office walls throughout Park Bank's headquarters were displayed plaques entitled "Winners and Losers," which began:

The Winner is always a part of the answer.
The loser is always a part of the problem.
The Winner always has a program;
The loser always has an excuse.

Sadly, Park Bank had no adequate excuse when it collapsed in early 1986. In retrospect, though Jacobs was trying simply to succeed under impossible conditions, rather than to prove him-

There's a name for the executive success syndrome: "encore anxiety."

self, he defined what he calls the Principle of Defective Observation:

> Our human observation is defective because each of us finds it necessary to interpret events we encounter and data we receive in ways that enhance our self-image and stabilize our perception of the universe. To that end, we search out and embrace information supporting our peculiar worldview. We exclude, refuse to gather, and refuse to recognize conflicting data.

Some years ago the term "myopia" was popularly used to describe the nearsightedness of business leaders—that is, their inability, or unwillingness, to take a long-term view. However, self-inflicted crises are often caused by a different perceptual flaw: hyperopia—the inability to see what is happening right under our noses. It's a symptom of what's been called the "CEO disease," and it's caused by an excessive application of money, perks, and power. Whatever you do, don't catch it.

Chapter Ten

Coping and Growing: A Self-Renewal Process

At the turning point of the movie *Annie Hall,* Alvy Singer (played by Woody Allen) says, "A relationship, I think, is like a shark. You know, it has to constantly move forward or it dies. I think what we have on our hands is a dead shark." Likewise, successful managers have to keep their work relationships and themselves constantly moving forward. They have to invest in their futures.

But what if you are stuck? How can you worry about the future when the present is closing in from every direction? First comes the need to cope. A new manager may be sandwiched between an unsympathetic supervisor and recalcitrant direct reports who could not care less about an approaching deadline. An experienced manager may be plateaued in an excruciatingly boring, dead-end assignment or trying to dig out from a bottomless pit of problems that the previous manager neglected to mention. Wanting to be successful, how can such managers overcome the feeling of powerlessness on the slippery lower rungs of the career ladder? It's a long way to the top, and the ladder's getting shaky.

But even at the top life can be terrifying. Corporate psychiatric consultant Gerald Kraines estimates that about one-fourth of the CEOs he has encountered "can never savor their success, because they have to keep working harder." This is partly because, like many other successful people, they fear that their inadequacy will eventually be revealed for all the world to see.

The answer? First, stop taking yourself so seriously. Remember: The sun is the center of the universe, not you. And no one is perfect. So stop seeking perfection.

Writer Logan Pearsall Smith once claimed that "the indefati-
gable pursuit of an unattainable perfection, even though it consists in nothing more than in the pounding of an old piano, is
what alone gives a meaning to our life on this unavailing star."
Maybe so, but that relentless pursuit, coupled with the powerlessness that every organization provides from time to time, is also
what brings unrelenting stress. Incidentally, Smith much later
had second, more modest, thoughts. Two weeks before his death
a friend asked whether he had discovered the meaning of life.
"Yes," was his reply, "there is a meaning; at least, for me, there
is one thing that matters—to set a chime of words tinkling in the
minds of a few fastidious people."

Perhaps there is some comfort in that bumper sticker dictum,
"If all else fails, lower your standards." But I believe high standards are important, so long as they are in the realm of reality.

A long-retired friend who had succeeded at several careers
once told me his version of the meaning of life. "Our mission,"

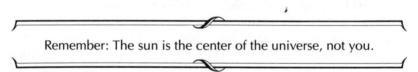

Remember: The sun is the center of the universe, not you.

he said, "is to entertain the angels. They are always looking down
on us. Sometimes they think they're watching a tragedy, only to
be surprised by a scene of high comedy. Or, expecting a farce,
they suddenly view a calamity of unbearable sadness. It's your
job not to bore the angels."

Since hearing that droll but profoundly useful explanation,
I've found it easier to handle the vicissitudes of life simply by
distancing myself and looking at life through those angels' eyes.
In today's high-tech heaven, angels can readily flip channels. So
whenever I hear a celestial "click," I know I've bored the angels.
And probably everyone else.

Work should be enjoyable and entertaining. Those who
achieve perspective find it so. Robert A. Beck, former chairman of
Prudential Insurance Company of America, put it this way:

> I think it's a shame that so many people live and die
> with the music still in them. . . . We spend so much of

our time working, why not have fun at it? Why not feel the thrill of getting something done, of winning, of being in front of the pack?

Irving S. Shapiro, as Du Pont's CEO, agreed:

Some people marvel at the energy I put into my work. What they don't understand is that this is not a job in the sense of having to go to work. It's a great experience. . . . My work represents a chance to accomplish things—to make things happen.

Handling Pressure: Is There a Magic Bullet?

How to handle the unremitting pressures of responsibility? Curiously, many managers try to cope by an astonishing variety of Band-Aid approaches. How about a customized relaxation tape? You can even take it on vacation, along with your mobile phone, fax, and laptop computer.

Kenneth R. Dubuque, chairman of Mellon Bank Corp.'s Mellon Bank (Maryland) Unit, used to spend his vacations tracking orangutans in the jungles of Borneo or checking out kangaroos in the Australian outback. He says, "Now [that I'm CEO] it's even more important that I be within earshot, so even getting a long weekend is going to be tough for me." But, he adds, long weekends are not enough.

To get away from your job *and* the fax machine, you could go on a cattle drive. In 1988, the Trammell Crow Co. awarded a dozen top performers a ten-day experience of herding 1,000 cows 75 miles. The company's newsletter later captioned a group photo of the cattle herders this way: "Moving cattle is a team effort, and team effort is what Trammell Crow is all about." But Trammell Crow's team efforts are also about leasing real estate, and there was real estate still to be leased after the cows came home.

Or, if getting away from it all does not appeal to you, then how about an inner journey? Instead of a Band-Aid, how about some emotional blood letting? Dallas's Timberlawn Psychiatric Hospital offers a four-week program for "high-functioning individuals" (for which read CEOs and others of that ilk) during

which each has access to at least two psychiatrists. Dr. Mark In-
terberg, who founded this program in 1987, recognizes that during the program, the VIP guests must be allowed to have access
to their telephones as well as to the psychiatrists.

If you wish to dig still deeper, psychiatrists Rick Weinberg
and Larry Mauksch of the University of South Florida offer "fam-
ily-of-origin therapy." In structured workshops you can explore
whether you have mistaken your company chairman for your
stepfather. Or whether, being the firstborn in a large family, you
protect your people as though they were your younger siblings.
According to Dr. Weinberg, "For many executives, it's a real
'Aha!' experience. They may have acknowledged difficulty with
their colleagues, but they've never looked at it this way before." I
suppose not.

These Five-Year Plans Really Worked

Professional help, of course, can be helpful, and for some it is
essential. For most of us, however, *self*-help is crucial, too.

During my first three years at a fast-growing, multinational
corporation, I held nine overwhelmingly challenging assign-

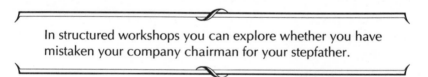

In structured workshops you can explore whether you have
mistaken your company chairman for your stepfather.

ments. Before I could master one job, I was given another. Anyone who has been given more responsibility than he or she can
handle knows that this is only half the story. For outside your
work life there are the strains of trying to be a decent spouse and
parent.

Failing at everything all at once can give you a feeling of profound inadequacy. At such times you have two choices: You can
try to cope, or you can walk away. Again, a little perspective
helps. You are neither the first nor the last to be in such a predic-
ament. Nor is stress confined to the executive suite. Indeed, studies have shown that the most stressful jobs are those of policemen
and inner-city teachers. Right behind them, according to one

study, are air traffic controllers, fire fighters, medical interns, assembly-line workers, and waiters. And middle managers were found to have about the same stress level as salespeople and lawyers. If they can cope, you can cope.

So it's *time* to cope. And you must do so in your own way. At the time I found myself *most* stretched, which was a few years later, I did two things. First, I headed for the Bahamas. There, with my wife beside me, the sun baked my brain and cleared my vision. Surprisingly, the company did not fall apart.

After returning to work, I approached the larger problem of the future by developing a primitive system of life planning. Taking a large sheet of paper, I listed in the left column my age in five-year intervals. Then I labeled three columns along the top of the page: strains, goals, and accomplishments. Thinking back to age 5, I reflected on what was probably bothering me as a young boy, what I then hoped would happen in the future, and just what—if anything—I had accomplished by that age. I did the same for ages 10, 15, and so on. Looking at what I'd written, I gained a much-needed perspective.

Then I took the plunge, asking myself what I wanted to accomplish during the *next* five years, including precisely how I'd change the situation I was in. I've stuck with this system and recently filled out the chart for age 65. Looking back at sixty years of strains and gains has been illuminating.

One finding that was surprising at first but, on reflection, totally predictable was this: With few exceptions, I had achieved my five-year goals. But each success brought new, self-inflicted stresses. Overcoming these, I then set new goals, and so on. I don't necessarily recommend this approach to you, but I do recommend that you find your own way of gaining perspective about your work life, your larger life, and their interrelationship.

Wait for Change—Or Make It Happen?

According to Socrates, the unexamined life is not worth living. Still, the unlived life is not worth examining. In *The Seasons of a Man's Life*, Daniel J. Levinson reports his longitudinal study of the lives of forty men whose ages ranged from 35 to 45. After probing their childhood and adolescent experiences, Levinson's team observed the subjects' transition through early and middle adulthood.

In the course of their study the researchers discovered a factor that plays a powerful, pervasive role in men's lives. Levinson called this the "Dream." Whatever the nature of a young man's Dream, he takes on the developmental task of better defining it and finding a way to live out the Dream. (Beyond the scope of Levinson's study was the woman's Dream, which may be more complex.) If our Dream fails to come true, we must make a major life adjustment. But if it *does* come true, what then? Fulfillment is never enough. So we create another Dream, then another, and still another. Throughout life there must be adjustment. Life is about change.

And so should work be. As a manager you have three tasks. First, to cope with yourself—to take control of your life. Failing this, you cannot succeed as a manager. Second, to cope with your responsibilities and the changes that they bring. But for real success there is a third task. To *create* change. Change in your organization. More important, change in yourself. You must make a commitment to continuously renew yourself.

Managers who understand this know that past experience is a two-edged sword. Whenever you find yourself making some automatic knee-jerk response to a problem, just because that's the way you solved a similar problem before, recognize that your much-vaunted experience is limiting you. And your organization.

If your vacations become the same old routine, year after year, and your social milieu consists of the same old people, recognize that you have settled in. And settled for the status quo. This is not to say that that continuity and stability have no virtue. We need to keep up with old friends and to be comfortable in familiar settings. But too much familiarity breeds content.

One of my early mentors stressed something he called "royal discontent." Even if you get to the top, he said, don't preside like a king. And if you have to act like a czar, he said, choose Peter the Great. A creator of change.

The best executives I know are change makers. They're imbued with intellectual curiosity. They want to know what makes things work. What the relationship is between this and that. They are excited by ideas. They read widely and deeply. Their interests are incredibly diverse, their lives rich and balanced. Balanced at work and in their home lives, they've achieved that rare equilibrium between the two. Their actions thunder their belief that life is not so much about themselves as it is about others. And they are possessed of an abundance of deep relationships with an amazing variety of people.

But as I said earlier, there are all sorts of managers, and all sorts of CEOs. I knew one CEO who was so comfortable with herself, and fond of fun, that she was irreverent and playful even at the most serious times of crisis. And quite a different one, still driven at age 78 by his conviction that he has never lived up to his father's measure. Yet both were successful, inspirational, top-drawer leaders. One quality they shared was their ability to change and to grow, to try new things, to take personal as well as corporate risks.

What does this mean to you? Only you can figure this out. And if you plan to be successful, this is as good a time as any to take stock of yourself. To look at yourself and your organization with that attitude of royal discontent. And to turn over not just a new leaf but a whole new chapter. Title it "Change."

Chapter Eleven

Going Global:
How to Become a
World-Class Manager

In 1967, Marshall McLuhan credited electronic interdependence with having recreated the world in the image of a global village. Over the next twenty-five years, economic interdependence remade it again, this time in the *reality* of a global shopping mall, or bazaar.

Today, products of virtually every American company are competed with by overseas competitors. And many are produced in not one, but several, foreign countries. Consumers can no longer be sure of a product's nation of origin or who (and of what country) owns a familiar service organization. Professor Robert Reich of the Kennedy School points out that an Italian-designed sports car, financed in Japan and assembled in Indiana, Mexico, and France, may employ advanced electronic components invented in New Jersey and fabricated in the Far East. Honeywell chairman and CEO James J. Renier claims, "We can bid something in the U.S., spec it in France, buy [parts] in Kuwait, and deliver it anywhere in the world."

The recent U.S. export boom, led by such companies as Boeing, General Electric, and 3M, illustrates a growing degree of American success in foreign markets. And such success is not limited to the largest corporations. Many small and mid-size companies have become competitive in foreign lands.

Still, you'd never guess how interconnected the world has become by talking with a typical domestic middle manager. To most, and surprisingly to many American CEOs, foreign customs and customers are just that. Foreign. Yet every day inexorable, centrifugal nationalistic forces are creating new markets. Meanwhile, centripetal economic forces are creating great trading blocs. In the coming era of the new world *dis*order, managers who prepare themselves through foreign studies and overseas experience will have an edge on those who don't. As the great tectonic plates of economic power shift and grind, markets will also markedly change. And it is change that creates opportunity.

But how do you become an internationalist, and when do you start? If as CEO you find you're less than *au courant* in matters international, it's still not too late to start an intense program of learning through travel, reading, and being expertly coached. But the best time to start is when you're young. High school and college students who have availed themselves of international exchange programs already have an edge on their peers. As do those who've tasted the excitement of foreign travel in other ways.

Leslie M. Schweitzer, founder and president of Schweitzer & Associates Trading Company, says this:

> To me there has always been glamour associated with international trade. Perhaps it was from the stories that as a child I used to seek out in the city library on ancient traders of China and Russia. There were tales of danger, intrigue, pirates, gold, romantic casbahs. I knew that that was the life for me—to be a Mata Hari from a small town in Kansas or the chairman of a vast giant empire of international trading houses headquartered in Peking. While my school chums dreamed of becoming Miss America or Doris Day or marrying Ricky Nelson, I dreamed of travel and exotic meeting rooms and first-class Pan Am flights and limousines. . . .
>
> No one knew better than my mother that not very many little girls from Osage City, Kansas, created international business empires unless they at least passed over the county line. She made sure I had that opportunity. Mexico, Europe, Russia, all before turning sweet sixteen. . . .
>
> Luck and timing had a lot to do with the way life has turned out, but it has also been the ability to leap at

an opportunity and take a chance. The risk taking, the truly sometimes frightening adventures, the loneliness, the sleepless nights are not for everyone. And the glamour really never was quite as I had imagined. I never met anyone quite like the heros in those books. Pan Am went bankrupt and jetlag was just as bad in first class as in coach. But still I love the business. . . . Don't get the impression that any of this has been easy. . . . The globalization of American business is incredibly expensive and risky and full of failure, but try we must.

For Schweitzer, as for Dorothy in *The Wizard of Oz*, it isn't Kansas anymore. Nor can it be for managers who lack her global outlook and experience. Not if they wish to succeed in today's business environment. But what can you do to make up for this lack?

They've Done Their Homework— Have You Done Yours?

Foreigners usually have a head start in international business because, in most cases, they know more about our culture than we can hope to know about theirs. American culture is seen everywhere, through CNN, American movies, even soap operas. And the U.S. market is so large and affluent that thousands of companies from every industrialized nation now successfully compete here.

Over the years, foreign executives by the thousands have rotated back and forth between work assignments in the United States and their home countries. This has resulted in a widespread knowledge of American social and business practices throughout the industrialized world. In contrast, for all but the most internationalized American executives, even the basics of foreign languages, customs, and markets are but vaguely understood. Yet visiting executives of our foreign competitors often understand even the nuances of our milieu. So, starting badly from behind, the single most important key to success overseas is serious homework.

But this kind of homework can't all be done at home. Young

managers should seek assignments requiring international travel and, if possible, overseas posts. The earlier the better.

Unlike leading Japanese firms such as Mitsubishi and NEC, which consider success in foreign assignments essential to fast-trackers' careers, many American companies handle returning older expatriates poorly. Despite their need for seasoned executives with foreign experience, American companies often fail to capitalize on such talent. Out of sight, out of mind. Senior executives would be wiser to seek a U.S.-based assignment that includes responsibility for some foreign operations rather than an overseas assignment per se.

Though English has become the international language of business, economist Paul McCracken observes, "For Americans,

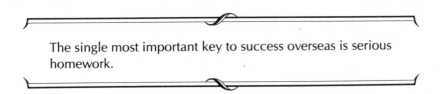

The single most important key to success overseas is serious homework.

English is a great language for buying but not so good for selling."

It's not so good either for visits to potential overseas partners. Foreign businesspeople, especially younger ones, put great effort into learning English. And in some countries English has become a required second language in school. Japan's ANA flights from Tokyo to the United States provide passengers with instructional English-language audiotapes to prepare them for specific needs such as renting a car or checking into a hotel. Japanese executives already fluent in English typically spend their flight time in preparing for their appointments. So they hit the ground running.

Contrast their on-board activity with that of a typical American businessman en route to Tokyo. I've noted that many glance over their itineraries but spend most of the time watching movies and having one too many drinks. It's still the unusual American who prepares for overseas trips by studying the language of the country to be visited.

Getting to Know You

Think globally, act locally. That's the common wisdom. But in many cultures, *feeling* ranks right up there with thinking. This is especially true in Eastern cultures, and unless you've become knowledgeable about a country's customs, you may miss this point completely.

No amount of rational analysis, however persuasively presented, can substitute for relationship building. Relations are built on emotions, not on facts. And to act locally, and *properly*, requires a deep immersion in that local foreign culture.

In visiting other countries, or even in their work assignments there, many American managers make the mistake of socializing primarily with other Americans, seeking out American clubs and living in American colonies. This may be great as a way of seeking relief from all the confusion, but it's not great for getting to know the territory.

I know one American who's worked in Brussels and Paris for decades but whose French-language skills still extend only to a menu. (Evidence that his deficiency stems not from a lack of language aptitude but from a lack of interest is that he knows the names of only a few people in his own organization.) Certainly some people have more aptitude for learning new languages than others. But even if you find this difficult or impossible, your efforts to do so will be appreciated, anywhere on the globe.

Eugenia Ulasewitz, named in 1991 president of the U.S. subsidiary of Galeries Lafayette, the French department store chain, believes she may have an edge in her efforts to learn French. Her five-year-old son Dennis is studying French in school. So in addition to being tutored, she says, "I'll probably be learning from him pretty soon." Enthusiasm is important. To paraphrase Samuel Johnson, if we are tired of Paris, we are tired of life.

The desire to learn is a powerful gift when traveling or working overseas. A great deal can be learned just from observing how others do business there, and much of this is directly transferable to your own business. By looking through others' eyes we can see better through our own. Intellectual curiosity is also a great asset in going international. Executives sufficiently possessed of it naturally seek to explore new environments and to understand cultural nuances and the history behind them. Managers lacking this gift must study long and hard.

Before visiting any country for the first time, learn some rudimentary phrases. Note what newsworthy events are taking place. Study its history and culture. Read some of its literature. Seek coaching in social and business protocols by someone who has lived there. Memorize the pronunciation of names of those you expect to meet. If the trip is an important one, order business cards with your name and title in English on one side and in the country's language on the other. And, importantly, arrange to be introduced within that country by as prestigious a person as you can find (prestigiousness as viewed by those in the host country, of course).

While you're there, reserve time for sightseeing with an informed guide. Go to concerts, the opera, the ballet. Visit art museums. In many countries even chief executives are deeply knowledgeable about their country's culture and, for that matter, contemporary American art and literature as well. By going this extra mile you can set yourself apart from other American CEOs.

Seated in an elegant club across the table from a European chief executive, remember that shoptalk is considered gauche. And you may find that golf anecdotes just won't sustain your end of the conversation through the final course. By becoming culturally literate, you'll set yourself apart in your company as well.

A recent survey by Dunhill Personnel Systems found that though U.S. firms have established successful trade and financial relationships overseas, for the most part American managers feel

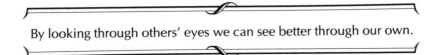

By looking through others' eyes we can see better through our own.

uncomfortable in the international arena. Respondents perceived themselves and their American peers as lacking adequate language facility, cultural understanding, and sufficient global business information. I cannot overemphasize the cultural factor. For example, many a gaffe has been made through the giving of inappropriate gifts—a serious matter in many countries. As an ignorant American you'll be forgiven many mistakes. But those who continue to breach foreign etiquette will be seen, correctly, as both insensitive and lacking in judgment.

In short, successful competition on a global scale requires managers, including CEOs, to do their homework thoroughly. In some parts of the world you may be surprised by how thoroughly your foreign counterparts have done theirs. You may find competitors or potential partners in the Far East who know more about your industry, your company, and you than you thought possible.

When they are with you in person, they'll take your measure in many ways. By your knowledge. Your preparedness. The appropriateness of your attire. The jokes you tell (or, preferably, your reluctance to tell jokes in a culture strange to you). Your listening skills. Your respect for their culture. The quality of the people around you, even your interpreter. Your goals as they perceive them. (Are you interested in quick profit, or in a long-term relationship?) Your tenacity. Your sensitivity, and your patience. Especially your patience. Don't bother going to China, or even Japan, if you're not in it for the long haul. And be prepared to spend time—a long time—building personal and corporate relationships, especially in the Far East or in the republics of the former Soviet Union.

Becoming World-Class

In recent years the term "world class" has been applied to describe products that are in demand throughout the world. American jazz and rock'n'roll. French wines. Japanese cars. CNN and MTV. Belgian chocolates. Russian vodka. Disney, Hermes, and Sony.

World-class companies know how to compete in today's world of instant communication and supersonic travel. Only weeks after the fall of the Berlin Wall, Coca-Cola entered the German Democratic Republic. Four months later, the East Germans were buying roughly one million cases of Coke per month. Anthony J. F. O'Reilly, chief executive of H. J. Heinz Company, said the following:

> Such episodes convey the prospect of not just a Euro-consumer but a global consumer. We may soon find that

a German student has more in common with a Canadian student or a Japanese student than he does with a German businessman. The significance of consumer stratification across national lines should not be lost on retailers, manufacturers, or marketers. It has not been lost on Heinz.

The reason that this has not been lost on Heinz is that O'Reilly is a world-class CEO. Equally at home in Beijing as in his Pittsburgh headquarters or his Dublin birthplace, after serving as CEO of the Irish Dairy Board and as managing director of the Irish Sugar Company, he formed a joint venture with H. J. Heinz and then led Heinz's U.K. company before becoming, in 1979, CEO of the entire multinational company. But it is not just O'Reilly's international experience that makes him a world-class executive. That is the least of it. Rather, he's a world-class CEO in the same sense that certain rare products from one country or another are world-class products. One associate says, "People hold Tony in awe because he's blessed with so many extraordinary abilities. He walks into a room and something changes."

CEOs of extraordinary quality don't require glamorous products to become world class. Ken Iverson, CEO of Nucor Corporation, showed the steel industry that workers in rural America can produce steel of the highest quality and at internationally competitive prices. James R. Houghton transformed what was a rather pedestrian glass company, Corning, into a high-technology growth firm with a global presence.

Stanley Gault, passed over as CEO by GE's board in favor of Jack Welch, went on in 1980 to become chief executive of Rubbermaid, then a stodgy producer of kitchen products. In addition to extending the company's lines of business (into toys, toolboxes, outside furniture, and many other products), he grew the core business dramatically. For example, its humble dustpan now sells by the millions all over the globe. When Gault retired from Rubbermaid, he became chief at troubled Goodyear Tire & Rubber, which he's now getting into shape to compete successfully with the Michelins and Bridgestones of the world.

In a world whose economy is increasingly fluid and churning, managers at all levels (and certainly CEOs) who seek real success must strive to become world-class managers. This implies the highest quality, reliability, and universality. It also implies adaptability and durability. But at the end of the day, world-class executives, like world-class products, earn their reputation by their ability to succeed against, and amongst, the best, wherever in the world the best may be.

Some things never change. Whether you're marketing in Hong Kong, managing in Germany, or manufacturing in Buffalo or Brazil, your people need to know you care about them and their opinions. They need to understand your direction and help to shape it. And they need quality—*real* quality—of leadership.

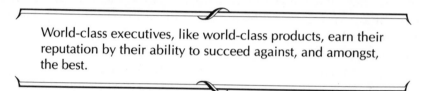

World-class executives, like world-class products, earn their reputation by their ability to succeed against, and amongst, the best.

No nation holds a monopoly on excellence in people. So as a CEO (or a manager at any level) you now have two choices. Either do what it takes to become world-class. Or watch the rest of the world go by.

Chapter Twelve

Manage *by* the Bottom Line—Or *to* It?

Let's start out by agreeing on something noncontroversial. Let's agree that making a profit is not the purpose of your business.

Not everyone would agree with this, of course, but I am sure you do. After all, you defined the purpose of your business through the planning process. Remember? You asked what business your organization should be in, and how it could succeed in that business. By answering those questions, you settled on your business's purpose. It's not that making a profit is an insufficiently noble cause. It's just that defining your organization's purpose as making money would not be very helpful—unless you're in the business of counterfeiting.

Profit is an outcome, not a goal. Indeed, Peter Drucker has described profitability not only as not the purpose of a business, but a limiting factor to it. Profitability is a test of a business's viability. And unless a company makes an adequate profit, the business will not sustain itself over time. Similarly, unless nonprofit organizations create surpluses, they won't be around either. The profit, or surplus, must cover the unexpected failures of your plan to pan out. And if your organization is to grow, profit may be needed for investment in its future, though outside financing may serve as a temporary substitute.

CEOs who ignore the bottom line, or think it will simply take care of itself, may have a surprise or two in their future. But at the other extreme, those who manage *by* the bottom line or by any other form of number crunching may end up getting crunched in the process. Though leaders never manage by the numbers, you can't manage without them, either.

Every organization needs strong financial management. I've always placed great importance on having the best chief financial officer I could find. What you need is a person with a broad outlook, one whose vision extends beyond financial statements to include, even emphasize, the customer. Such a CFO can help you in innumerable ways to improve your company's financial results.

Over the long term, of course, these results are influenced even more by you. So even if your background is in finance, find yourself an outstanding CFO. The most successful chiefs, even of small companies, recruit the best financial expertise they can find. In larger, more mature companies, there's also a need for a treasurer, to deal with the management of cash and of debt, bank relationships, and other critical functions. You need to be freed up to work on what goes *into* the financial statements and *into* the treasury. A capable CFO with whom you have a good relationship will bring to your attention the numbers you most need to see. And there are plenty of such numbers. Just try not to kill the messenger whenever your CFO brings you bad news.

Still, for some CEOs the financial bottom line is the only bottom line. That's all they see, and that's what they manage by. For many years ITT's Harold Geneen was considered—though perhaps unfairly—as the prototypical bottom-line manager. At ITT, one major innovation, as he called it, was his edict that comptrollers in every division of the company submit their financial reports directly to him at New York headquarters. Naturally, there was an immediate outcry from the division managers, who charged that he was turning their financial chiefs into spies for the home office. He denied this completely, saying instead that the procedure was for the sake of improved communications. *Upward* communications, he must have meant.

This is not to say that you shouldn't study financial reports. To the contrary, you'll need to dig deeply both into and behind their figures. But they are just figures, not reality.

Creating Budgets You Can Live With

The budget, while unglamorous, is the most basic of financial instruments. Yet, despite its simplicity, it is badly misunderstood.

Many managers consider it an instrument of control. After all, someone called the controller helped your line people to put their budgets together and watches those budgets like a hawk.

If your organization's level of sophistication has reached the point where you have someone called a budget director, you may mistakenly think that someone with that title is actually directing the budget. The truth, of course, is that control of your organization comes from the competence and integrity of your managers and from the relationship you have with them. And it is they who are responsible for creating their budgets and for achieving the results to meet them.

Some years ago, when commercial aircraft lacked electronic means to be positively identified by air traffic controllers on the ground, the controllers responsible for their safe landing had to make judgments about the pilots themselves. Some pilots, eager to land and go home after a long flight, would misrepresent their plane's position, reporting themselves miles nearer to the runway than they were. By doing this they hoped to be assigned an earlier landing slot than they would otherwise have been given, based on their actual position. The airport-based controllers, lacking reliable data but quite familiar with this game, had to calibrate the reported positions by an intuitive credibility factor based on earlier experience with the particular pilots. (Luckily, passengers didn't know this was going on.)

Dealing with managers during the budget-preparation phase requires that similar judgments be made. Does the unit's manager have a history of overoptimism? Or of "low-balling" budgeted results? Are these results bought into by the people within the unit who have to achieve these results? Or do some of these results seem to be imposed from the top? Even before budgets are prepared, there must be agreement on a variety of economic assumptions. And most important, the figures must be closely attuned to the realities of the market and its anticipated trends.

In their preliminary stages, budgets are at best estimates that are based on realistic expectations. Through careful review and negotiation, however, they must become commitments. Unless they do, you'll be renegotiating, instead of managing, the future. For the purpose of the budget is to provide a way to measure actual results against the results your people committed themselves to achieve. In this way the budget helps to reallocate resources, for it is the variance between the actual and the expected that will trigger attention and suggest remedial actions. Periodic forecasts along the way may bring your expectations more into line with reality. But even when variances between budgeted results and actual results are great, this discrepancy should not be used as justification to revise the budget.

Are You Looking at the Right Numbers?

Earlier it was pointed out that the budget is a fundamental financial instrument, and so it is. But just as fundamental, though not as grounded in reality, are the figures contained in your strategic plan.

Indeed, if you've been planning well, the figures in the budget should have a direct linkage with those in the plan. Yet the budgeted figures are closer to reality, having been tempered by much experience and further modified by trends underway or clearly foreseen. Once the budgets are negotiated, if all goes well (and it often does not), your monthly income-and-expense statements should closely track your budget. And if all goes *very* well, you'll be making a profit. On paper, that is.

A paper profit, however, isn't going to do you much good if your company lacks the wherewithal to stay in business. An important issue at all times is the financial condition of your organization. What does the balance sheet look like? Are your assets sufficiently liquid to keep the business going? What's happening to your accounts receivables and bad debts? Are your payables sufficiently current? Can your debts be adequately serviced? Are shareholders' dividends ensured? What is happening to various important ratios? Your creditors will be keeping their eye on the ratio of your current assets and liabilities as a test of your company's solvency, and your investors will be looking at your debt-to-equity ratio. Too much debt means excessive interest payments, and too little may retard your growth. All kinds of conclusions can be gleaned from close analysis of your financial reports.

Still, it's easy to be fooled. After all, budgets at best convey a theoretical view of the future. And accounting reports convey only an approximate view of the past. Worse, each such report is merely a snapshot in time. Next month's snapshot may be surprisingly, even disastrously, different. Meanwhile, cash is flowing into and especially out of your company every hour.

Especially in start-up and rapidly growing companies, you'd do better by simply keeping your eye on the till. If you do, you'll soon note that the outflow of cash is much more rapid than its inflow.

In 1991, ninety-three U.S. companies whose annual sales exceeded $100 million were enjoying growth rates of 50 percent or higher. Six had been growing at rates exceeding 200 percent annually. Managing such rapid growth is like trying to harness a whirlwind. As rapid growth occurs, there is an immediate need for more of everything. More people, more material, more equipment, more computing power. This means more cash. The Niagara of outflowing funds must be replenished. And to reduce borrowing needs, you'll need to focus on the nitty-gritty of receivables and collections.

Because the goal is not just growth (in these kinds of compa-

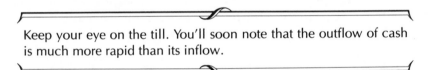

Keep your eye on the till. You'll soon note that the outflow of cash is much more rapid than its inflow.

nies that's already happening almost beyond belief) but *profitable* growth, the stale numbers of your financial reports may not be a useful snapshot at all. You might as well be looking at a daguerreotype. Instead, it's time to manage by cash flow. Who's looking after collections?

In a small company, even the CEO might have to attend to this. A friend of mine, the founder and chief executive of a three-year-old firm in Dallas whose volume exceeds $10 million, did just that by asking the right questions and getting involved herself. While making marketing calls on her largest accounts, she also made it a point to meet the individuals most influential in paying her company's bills. One happened to be the secretary to a chief accountant. By explaining the importance of prompt payments to a company short of cash, she was able to persuade the secretary to move her company's invoices regularly from the bottom of the stack to the top. The consequence? What had been 60-day payments miraculously became 10-day payments.

During this period of rapid growth, this CEO focused her attention on three critical areas: customers, employees, and cash. To ensure a rapidly growing company's future, cash is essential. With many new employees on board, training is vital. So is the hiring of new people, if quality of service is to be maintained for a growing customer list. And during such a time, chances are that customers simply aren't getting the kind of quality care they need, because the work force is stretched to its capacity. Customer calls from the CEO can provide that added personal touch needed to keep the customers happy.

In the case of the Dallas company, the CEO managed to combine all three concerns by taking along a new manager on her calls, thereby orienting the manager to the business from the customers' standpoint. And while she was at the customers' offices, she dropped in to charm whoever was responsible for paying her bills.

But even careful cash management is not enough during periods of rapid growth. Attention must also be focused on planning. In a fast-growing company, chances are that the assumptions that went into the plan are no longer valid. So it's time to replan.

These days, however, most companies are not experiencing hypergrowth. Instead, many are struggling just to make ends meet. If you're CEO of a company that's barely making it or, worse, starting to fail, the lack of cash may also be a problem, a serious one. But that may be the least of your worries. What you probably lack more than anything else are customers. Here you might want to listen to Peter Drucker once more. If making money is not the purpose of your business, then just what is? Drucker points out that the only valid definition of business purpose is *to create a customer*.

As CEO, you must lead the way in creating customers. You may need to do a lot of things concurrently, such as stopping the hemorrhaging of cash. Some CEOs think that under difficult conditions it's time to beat on their managers and exhort the troops. Of course, this is exactly the wrong thing to do, unless you want them to do whatever it is they've been doing wrong twice as fast.

Or, you might think it is time to go to the bank. Maybe a little borrowing will help to tide the company over. But what bank will lend money to a failing company? Without a solid business plan, significant borrowing is out of the question. Instead, it's time to link every activity of your firm to your current customers' needs and to find new ones.

Despite the fact that time may be running out, you'll still need to take time to plan, to make a financial inventory. But more important, you'll need to make an inventory of your organization's strengths and weaknesses, opportunities and challenges. You can learn a lot about its weaknesses just by listening to your customers. So if you've suddenly been given responsibility for running a failing company, the most productive action you can take is to start a series of crash planning sessions in which you link the plan's assumptions strongly to the customers' needs and, by so doing, begin to turn your company into a market-driven organization. Cost cutting, or preferably cost management, is essential. But by itself, this will simply contribute to a spiralling downturn over time.

Cutting Expenses: The Solution or the Problem?

Whereas chief executives must manage *to* the bottom line, those who manage *by* it too often concentrate on the wrong part of the financial statement—the expense line. It's easy enough to cut expenses. The wave after wave of downsizings of the 1980s and early 1990s give solid testimony to this fact. Indeed, today there are not only articles and books on downsizing but a whole half-billion-dollar industry called outplacement, ready for a fee to help us do it right.

Business writer John Thackrey describes the process this way:

A CEO calls his middle managers to a meeting on the company grounds. After making a short speech about the need for running "mean and lean," he gives a signal and a firing squad dispatches 15 percent of the assembled managers. Six months later he calls the survivors out again and another 15 percent are similarly eliminated. To those who are left, the CEO then says: "OK, now let's go out and kill the competition."

The trouble is, there may not be enough of the right people left to face the competition successfully. Worse, the competition may have hired the best people you let go. During the 1980s' merger-and-acquisition frenzy, many companies began to deal with people by the numbers. Though CEOs seldom failed to celebrate the importance of their people in annual-report rhetoric, they used terms like "headcount" to describe them when the crunch came, as though human beings were fungible commodities. Often, managing by the numbers is simply a symptom of short-term thinking.

The more successful CEOs concentrate on, and improve, the *income* line by working with their people to develop products and services that capture competitors' customers and create new ones. Obviously, expenses cannot be overlooked because today only the highest-quality, *lowest-cost* product can succeed in the global market. Still, growth comes from increasing income, not from reducing expenses.

Despite the importance of the *top line*—the income line—there are still many bottom-line executives. One of the most in-

> Often, managing by the numbers is simply a symptom of short-term thinking.

tense is reported to be Laurence A. Tisch, chairman and CEO of CBS. After a long and highly successful investment career, he began investing in CBS in 1985 and, through an intriguing and aggressive approach, replaced Thomas Wyman as CEO the following year. Though the CBS board named him as acting chief executive, with an understanding that his position would be only temporary, at this writing he is still running CBS. And according to all accounts, he's still managing it by the bottom line.

By repeatedly paring CBS's staff and divesting major parts of the company, Tisch managed to alienate employees and CBS affiliates alike, earning the nickname "The Missile." By 1992, there were speculations that Tisch, more than five years into his job, had plans for CBS. Maybe big plans. But no one seemed sure as to whether those plans were to sell the shrunken network or just what. But those who knew him predicted that whatever decision he would reach would be reached by the numbers.

Numbers were all-important too to some of the takeover specialists of the 1980s. One highly placed executive in a large company now owned by one such takeover firm says this: "The word *people* is not in their vocabulary. As long as our numbers look good, they don't bother me. But God help me if they start looking bad."

How CEOs Can Help the Bottom Line

Still, while numbers are not all-important, they are *critically* important. Ignoring them invites disaster. The CEO whose company is acquired through a hostile takeover may have been doing a great job building the company's balance sheet but may not have given sufficient attention to shareholders' desires for dividends and growth. The chief executive of a company that fails may have been sedated by glowing reports of profitability but neglected to be sufficiently concerned about cash needs, market trends, or the need to invest in the future.

Having good financial reports and the ability to interpret and apply them effectively is essential to any business. And it is the ability to understand the interrelationships between the various financial statements that is key, particularly that between the balance sheet, the income statement, and cash flow reports. Within each of these, and other, reports—and behind their figures—lie important clues as to where you need to focus your attention. Still, all these taken together represent only a wide-angle snapshot in time. To ensure a healthy bottom line for the future, you'll also need statistical reports and analyses of great variety.

As chief executive, you have been empowered by your directors to control and allocate the company's resources. Only you, or someone to whom you've granted major authority, have the power to authorize, for example, the capital and operating expenditures required to move a product from its research phase to the market.

Watching the numbers while making such decisions is important. But it's even more important to understand the risks you're taking by doing this. Or, just as important, by not doing it. This requires a knowledge on your part not only of financial matters but of the human capabilities available to you. All the return-on-investment studies in the world can't make the decision for you.

Nevertheless, you need to know the probable return on investment in order to make the decision. But it is vital that you know the reality of what's happening—what's *actually* happening—within your organization. For example, who is responsible for the success of the product, and what is that person's track record? Successful executives learn to balance their time effectively between operational management and financial management.

Inevitably, the CEO will be judged in many ways. The most significant financial measure over time will be the market value of the company. This can be increased only through a consistent record of profitable growth, which in turn can come only through profitable operations, financial leverage, and astute cash management. Throughout a CEO's career, the constantly recurring questions should be these: "How can I best deploy my resources—human, physical, and financial? What are the best opportunities both for the short and long terms?"

As CEO you are the most influential (and the most expensive) human resource at your command. How should *your* talents be deployed? Ask yourself these questions: "Where can I make the most difference? How can I most favorably impact the bottom

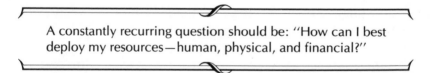

A constantly recurring question should be: "How can I best deploy my resources—human, physical, and financial?"

line?" Chances are the line that needs the most attention is the income line. How can you impact that?

In the end, your bottom line as CEO should not be just profit but the profitable growth of your company. And remember: Your job is one of leadership, not just management. So the best question is probably this: "How can I best *lead* my organization to achieve profitable growth?"

Chapter Thirteen

Corporate Culture: Ignore It at Your Peril

Here comes the soft stuff, you say. Vision and values. Rites and artifacts. Shared assumptions and beliefs. Heroes and tribal stories. In short, corporate culture.

Let's skip over this mushy stuff and get back to the bottom line, you say. But there is nothing soft or mushy about the focused team spirit of successful organizations. Visit any General Electric facility. Any IBM branch office. Any Wal-Mart store. Or note the difference in ambience of different airlines. Or the attitude expressed when you call one department store or another to get a billing error corrected. There are big differences between companies, and those differences can help—or hinder—a company's success. Your company's, too.

The company you have come to lead already has a corporate culture in place. But one way or another, deliberately or not, you will influence it by your thinking and your actions. And the longer you serve, the more profound (for better or worse) the cultural change will be. If you're still skeptical, then consider this: The effects you have on the corporate culture of your company will inevitably—if slowly—drop to your bottom line.

An organization's culture permeates the whole organization. It is invisibly managing the workplace even when you're not. And it's made manifest to the outside world by even the lowest-level employee. Because cultural change must start at the top, and reach the bottom, the task of changing a culture is not easy. Nor can it be done overnight.

Indeed, Professor Edgar H. Schein of the Sloan School of

Management at M.I.T., one of the foremost authorities in the field, believes it's quite possible that the *"only thing of real importance that leaders do is to create and manage culture* and that the unique talent of leaders is their ability to work with culture." In the long run this may be the part of your job that counts the most.

We've all experienced horror stories on airlines, times when we were treated like cattle or were just ignored by flight attendants who seemed to consider passengers' requests as unwarranted intrusions into their social lives. Have you noticed that some of these carriers are no longer around? In contrast, some airlines treat their passengers as paying customers. The attitudes of ticket agents and flight crews are driven by the attitudes and actions at the top.

Southwest Airlines, now a $1.5 billion company and one of the few leading airlines that are profitable, is led by chief executive Herbert D. Kelleher. Despite the rapid growth of the airline, Kelleher has been able to maintain a strong culture characterized by high productivity and intense staff loyalty.

SWA's senior executives spend one day each quarter sustaining the culture by working all jobs in the field and then later meeting to share their experiences. This provides close interaction among workers at all levels. Southwest's mission statement, aimed at its employees, not the public, is communicated in surprising ways. Once, for example, it arrived in sealed packages of Cracker Jacks. A great party giver, Kelleher has lined the halls of Southwest's Dallas headquarters with thousands of photographs of employees having fun. And he seems to be having the most fun of all. So do his passengers.

According to one airline analyst, "The work force is dedicated to the company. They're Moonies basically. That's the way they operate." But they're *not* Moonies. Instead, they're empowered workers who thrive in a company whose credo is that no individual team member is more important than any other.

How a Cultural Revolution Is Remaking General Electric

The General Electric Company has a long and distinguished history, going back to its founding in 1878 as The Edison Electric

Light Company. Over the years its leadership has changed many times. But by 1972, when Reginald Jones became chairman and CEO, its culture was well established and strong.

Jones described GE as a family. "We enjoy each other. We don't lose many in the family of GE. . . . We're so supportive of each other. We try desperately to save an individual who has failed, by placing him in a job that better matches his capacities . . . . We save many people." But on the negative side, Jones added that GE was seen (quite correctly) as one of the most financially conservative companies. He added that a foreign visitor had said that GE reminded him of "a staid old woman who looks both ways before going across the street."

During Jones's tenure, he made no attempt to revolutionize GE's culture. He worked "with the grain." But in 1973, he did publish some of his own beliefs in a document entitled "Management Style and Related Convictions." These included the need to minimize ambiguity, to do one's homework, to plan strategically, to know people as *individuals*, to be decisive, and (an important part of the GE culture) to put on the "company hat." For Jones this worked. He managed to turn around a great and financially troubled company and to leave it, nine years later, financially sound. And in the hands of a very different kind of CEO.

Jones had started as an accountant and auditor. Jack Welch, his successor, had begun as a chemical engineer. Welch, too, was a product of the GE culture. But unlike Jones, Welch decided to cut against the grain by developing new rules, insisting that GE's business units be in first, or at least second, position in their respective world markets. Welch then went to work on the challenging job of changing GE's culture.

He described communicating his vision and the atmosphere around that vision as "without question, the toughest job." But that was not the only tough job. Welch shed unsuccessful business units and unneeded people in such quantity that he earned the nickname "Neutron Jack." (So much for saving GE people.)

More important, he began shaking up the immense organization. To do so he used a variety of methodologies, including a technique called Work-Out. In Work-Out sessions, groups of GE employees spend two days together in an informal setting, thinking through how to improve their part of the business. On the third day they lob proposals for change at the manager responsi-

ble for that part of the business (and who is not privy to the discussions leading up to their proposals). The manager on the spot
has only three choices. To agree. To disagree. Or to give the date
by which he or she will have enough information to agree or disagree. The fact that the manager's own manager may be in the
room and not saying a word makes this process all the more pun-
gent.

Another technique for change at GE is called Best Practices,
which focuses on looking at the way other companies, across
widely disparate industries, handle such ordinary functions as
billing or shipping. A third, Process Mapping, is a process improvement methodology that draws on the ideas of customers
and suppliers as well as those responsible for the process internally. These and other culture-shattering approaches, each ap-
proved by and some developed with personal input from CEO
Jack Welch, are changing a lot of assumptions—and old ways of
doing business—at GE.

Still, nothing is easy. Though the business press gives GE
credit for writing the original book on management, and Welch
credit for rewriting it, hype is not always reality.

Friends at GE tell me, unsurprisingly, that Work-Out doesn't
always work out. And the process-change processes sound great
but frequently run into stone walls of resistance. Even so, General
Electric's culture is in a process of change. Many of its old values
will endure, but some of Welch's new values will be added.
Speaking up. Taking charge. Looking outside the company. Acting as an owner. Taking risks.

In making GE more participative, Welch too is taking a risk.
For as Rodger Bricknell, a General Electric power-systems execu-

> Though the business press gives GE credit for writing the original
> book on management, and Welch credit for rewriting it, hype is not
> always reality.

tive in Schenectady, implies, employee involvement, if taken sufficiently far, is impossible to turn off: "If you teach a bear to
dance, you'd better be prepared to keep dancing till the bear
wants to stop."

By 1992, Welch began to shed his "Neutron Jack" image by publicly affirming, in GE's annual report, his commitment to human values. Trust and respect between workers and managers, he said, were essential. No longer, he added, could GE tolerate "management styles that suppress and intimidate." Instead, managers should have "the self-confidence to empower others and behave in a boundaryless fashion." Clearly, Welch had decided to manage GE's culture in an open, hands-on way.

Take It From the Top

Empowerment. . . . Employee involvement. . . . Are these the keys to cultural change? Partly, but only partly. Employees can help define what needs to be done, but management must follow through. The real key, or tool, to cultural change is a commitment on the part of top management to be willing to change anything. And everything.

Members of the work force can identify the procedures, the rules, the processes that are holding them back. But you and your team then have to change them. No process and no structure can be considered holy writ, once it has been identified as an obstacle. That's why General Electric, to change its culture (and its results) is focusing on process, as well as—more recently—on values.

Where does corporate culture begin? In the case of Wal-Mart, which has a strong and recognizable culture, it began with founder Sam Walton's ideas, assumptions, and beliefs. And his incredible commitment.

Being so much younger than General Electric, Wal-Mart's culture is still influenced by Walton. In 1991, then age 73 and fighting an incurable bone cancer, Walton continued to fly his own twin-prop Cessna to visit stores. By that time Wal-Mart boasted 1,650 stores and dozens of Sam's Clubs. Yet, incredibly, Walton said, "Right now there are probably about 30 stores I've never been to and a bunch of others I haven't seen in more than a little while. I've got to get to 'em soon. I'm going to our first store opening in New Hampshire next week, and on the way I'm going to hit a store I've never been to up in Toledo."

More than just a great motivator, Walton kept an eye on everything. Quality. Expenses. "I don't want Wal-Mart going soft," he said to a longtime employee, "do you?" The folksy, friendly but dead-serious-about-the-customer culture of Wal-Mart was the creation of one man. Yet his successor, David D. Glass, is carrying on the Mr. Sam tradition. And no doubt he will influence the culture in ways as yet unseen. Still, the legacy of Sam Walton, who died in 1992, is indelible.

The founder of any organization has the seminal influence in creating an organization's culture. Entrepreneurs often (perhaps even typically) begin their businesses not just to make money, not just to provide a product or service, but to express themselves. And their values.

The fabled Stew Leonard's Dairy Store in Norwalk, Connecticut, has at its entrance a large stone into which is literally engraved both the founder's first rule, "The customer is always right," and rule #2, "If the customer is ever wrong, reread rule #1." These rules are Leonard's way to achieve competitive advantage, and they started with his own personal values. Similarly, the cultures of Apple Computer and Microsoft were created by the beliefs of Steve Jobs and William H. Gates 3rd, respectively, as was the culture of your favorite neighborhood pizzeria created by its founder.

Some years ago, a culture was defined as a "system of informal rules that spells out how people ought to behave most of the time." However, a culture goes far beyond rules. At its heart is a core of shared beliefs, for in such cultures employees know how to act without following rules. When emergencies arise, they rise to the occasion by acting on their beliefs, not by following rules.

Even giant companies were once tiny start-ups. What is now IBM, for example, was once just a ragtag collection of three small, undistinguished companies, known together as the Computing-Tabulating-Recording Company. According to Tom Watson, Jr., his father did not, in 1914, try to "move in and shake up the organization. Instead he set out to buff and polish the people who were already there and to make a success of what he already had."

Over the years the senior Watson built a culture based on his own beliefs. The first of these was respect for the individual. "This belief was bone-deep in my father," Watson, Jr., said in 1963, when he articulated the company's basic beliefs.

Twenty-five years earlier, one example of just how bone-deep this belief permeated IBM, and how widely, occurred in 1938 during the Nazi occupation of Czechoslovakia. A German soldier who had been an IBM manager in Germany was assigned to escort prisoners by rail. On the train, he recognized one as a former Czech branch manager. After creating a small ruckus, he restored order quickly, but not quickly enough to keep the prisoner from jumping unharmed from the train. In making that move he risked his life to save another's. That's how strong a corporate culture can be.

But the reign of the Watsons ended over 20 years ago. Since then there have been four successive CEOs. And while IBM still has a strong culture, the role of its basic beliefs has somewhat changed. And so, profoundly, has its culture.

The task of maintaining a founder's culture is not easy. And who says that it doesn't need changing? Even more difficult is the task of transforming and re-energizing the culture of a large company. Yet Jack Welch seems to be doing just that at General Electric, despite formidable obstacles. "We are trying to become a $60-billion global company with the fire and zest, the heart and soul of a start-up," he says.

Sometimes a Company Needs Shock Treatment

Whenever a radical change of culture is required, experts advise that the first step toward change is to "unfreeze" the organization's behavior by a variety of highly visible actions. Or, as Stanford Business School Professor Richard Pascale says, organizations need to be repeatedly *shocked* into change. Several new thrusts are needed to shock the organization sufficiently to change.

For example, after British Airways was privatized in 1982, its business needed to be redefined from *transportation* to *service* for the airline to become competitive. A whole series of new structures, new processes, new training, and new reward systems were introduced. Its process of change has required years, even with the assistance of highly qualified process consultants and considerable tenacity on the part of its then new CEO, Sir Colin Marshall. But the change is palpable to those who've flown regularly on the airline. The cultural message has become visible to passengers and employees alike.

Whirlpool Corporation, the world's leading producer of household appliances (or "white goods"), is currently going through cultural change not only in the United States but also overseas.

Jan Prising, president and CEO of Whirlpool International, considers fighting bureaucracy within the organization as one of his most essential tasks. Made up of several merged companies, Whirlpool now manufactures products in ten countries and markets them in forty-five. To compete successfully in the global market, the company created a worldwide program of quality improvement. This eventually involved (among other things) hundreds of task forces, each aimed at improving the quality of some specific product or service. And most were made up of groups of employees that included hourly workers.

Visiting a Whirlpool factory in Naples, Prising asked one of the hourly workers on a task force (none of whom had ever seen a corporate president before) how he felt about his involvement. The worker's reply was this: "Adesso, Io esisto" ("Now, I exist"). It is the emotional involvement of people deep within an organization that is essential to effective cultural change.

As chief executive you may choose to confirm your company's existing culture, or you may choose to transform it. (Or at least to try.) But the one thing you cannot do, if you hope to be successful, is to ignore it. If your behavior as chief contradicts the traditional values of the culture as understood by the work force, you'd better know what you're doing. Otherwise, you'll create mistrust, inconsistent behavior, and ultimately chaos.

Your task is particularly difficult—and important—if a merger or acquisition has taken place. That's when corporate cultures

> It is the emotional involvement of people deep within an organization that is essential to effective cultural change.

and their differences become most visible and, inevitably, most troublesome. Hostile takeovers, involving the victors and the vanquished, may produce intensely rivalrous cultures of sharply dif-

ferent values—causing the energies of the work force to be negatively, and inwardly, focused. Even the most friendly merger,
however, may fail if *you* fail to address the cultural differences that
any merger brings. An error often made by the CEO of an acquiring company is to ensure the acquired work force, or its managers, that "we don't plan to make any significant changes to your
operations." Such CEOs are destined to eat their smooth words
many times over. An even more serious error is to assume that
the acquired work force will easily digest and assimilate the values and unwritten rules of the acquirer—or be willing, or able, to
give up their own.

In heading up *any* company, you have no choice but to study
its culture carefully. You'll need to understand its values. If your
organization is doing well, you will want to identify those values
that are helping it move forward and then confirm and make
them visible by your own behavior, sometimes even by dramatic
behavior. But trying to enhance or change a corporate culture is a
tricky business. So call on expert organizational development advice even before you think you need it.

It All Starts With You

Especially when your company's results are plummeting, it's time
to look hard at what's wrong with its culture. Anecdotal evidence
gleaned through talking with your people will help provide insight, but there is no substitute for professionally administered
behavioral instruments. And there's no point in trying to change
a culture (even with the most qualified help available) unless *you*
know what *you're* trying to accomplish.

You *should* be trying to improve results, not just trying to
change behavior. Trying to change people's beliefs is difficult
enough even for people of the cloth. (And chances are you're not
a minister.) Peter Drucker reminds us that "culture—no matter
how defined—is singularly persistent." And he suggests that
changing culture is not necessarily going to change behavior,
much less yield the desired improvement and results. But any
change you make (or *try* to make) needs to be closely linked with
your strategy. In turn, your strategy must be linked to your customers' needs.

Consider also Mae West's advice: Anything that's worth doing is worth doing slowly. Do you think your company's in a crisis now? If you want to see a real crisis, try to force a cultural change on some arbitrary schedule. So give the matter some thought. Remember: Cultural change starts at the top, with the CEO. It is your behavior, more than any other factor, that sets the tone and thus affects the culture. Your *behavior*. Not what you say. Not what you think. Not what you hope. So start out by looking at yourself. Think about *your* "bone-deep" beliefs. About your actions and how others emulate them. Do you want your company to be more customer-driven? Then begin placing customers' needs consistently above your own. In fact, find out what their needs really are.

Sitting at the top, the CEO has as one part of his or her job the task and opportunity of seeing further into the distance. And seeing more clearly. Outside resources are more available to you than to anyone else within the organization. Calling on them is part of your job.

But in addition, sitting on that pinnacle makes you uniquely visible. So what you do and how you do it will have more effect on your company's culture—and its results—than any number of

> Start out by looking at yourself. Think about your "bone-deep" beliefs.

behavioral-science specialists or organizational-development consultants.

If in looking down from your pinnacle you conclude that your company's culture is just a mass of individuals operating on their own beliefs, not yours, then it's time for you to think about how your values connect to the company's history and to today's realities.

According to Max DePree, chairman and former CEO of Herman Miller, "The first responsibility of a leader is to define reality." Having done that, you might decide that changing a culture, or creating a new one, is the thing to do. If so, don't ever, ever try to do it alone. Cultural transformation is no job for an amateur. Get help. Remember, you're not an anthropologist. You're just the CEO.

Chapter Fourteen

Management Style: You've Gotta Be You

Like tropical plants and fruit flies, managers have been the object of microscopic scrutiny for many years, and various classifications have been postulated. Some managers are authoritarian, others participatory. Some are results-oriented, others process-oriented. Simplistic labels are applied to managers with differing "styles."

Michael Maccoby, for example, studied over 250 corporate managers and sorted them into four types: the craftsman, the jungle fighter, the company man, and the gamesman. James MacGregor Burns described leaders as transactional and transforming. Then there is the long-running debate as to whether managers and leaders are two different species of Homo sapiens, suggesting to some that managers are free to choose whatever style happens to be in fashion: "Let's see now. Those off-the-rack styles seem rather stale. Why not try a little mix-and-match? How about: Participative but still decisive. Sincere appearance. Stentorian voice. Great eye contact. And a touch of charisma around the edges. Nothing too obvious, though."

The elements of a management style can't be ordered from a catalog, however. So some budding executives choose a role

> Let's see now. A touch of charisma around the edges. Nothing too obvious, though.

model to imitate. I once knew an eager young assistant to a corporate chairman whom he decided to emulate. The chairman was a rugged individualist who enjoyed sailing, skiing, mountain climbing, and flying his own plane. Before long his obsequious young assistant became a skier, a sailor, a climber, and a flier. Soon his career too took flight. For a while, anyway. Then it soon lost altitude. Meanwhile, the former up-and-comer had lost the respect of his peers. Worse, he had lost himself by trying to become someone else, and he ended up a man in an empty suit.

This is not to say that role models are not important. In my career, I've been lucky to know several great men and women from whom I've learned much, just by watching them. Irving Shapiro admits that when he was chairman of Du Pont, he often tried to imagine what Walter Wriston (then Citicorp CEO) would have done in a particular situation and "would adapt that to my own style." And in these days of the so-called glass ceiling, women role models are important.

In 1991, when Debora de Hoyos was named managing partner of the 532-attorney, Chicago-based law firm of Mayer, Brown & Platt, letters and calls, many from strangers, came streaming in to her. "It perturbed me at first," she said. "I didn't think of myself as a symbol. I thought of myself as someone who has had a good professional experience." But, she added, "It was very important to a lot of people. One client called to say how pleased he was as a father of two daughters."

Similarly, black managers need black role models. In 1988, Bernard B. Beal joined with several partners to form M. R. Beal & Company, a rapidly growing, minority-owned investment bank on Wall Street, a community largely populated by white males. "There is no way that there is any advantage to being a minority firm in the buying and selling of securities," he said. "Nobody is going to sell a bond to you for one-eighth of a point less just because you're black." And he refers to what he calls a solid lucite ceiling: "It's worse than a glass ceiling, because at least you can break glass."

But role models, whether female or male, black or white, young or old, are meant to be learned from, not impersonated. To do so is self-limiting.

Just as self-defeating is any attempt to force yourself into some prescribed management style. Successful managers must demonstrate human qualities, which defy classification. Trying to stuff yourself into some pigeonhole is futile and, at the end, damaging. It is harmful to you through the unnecessary stress brought about by trying to play an unnatural role, and it is harmful to the organization by withholding from it parts of your intrinsic potential.

The only sensible advice is this: Be yourself. Remember, there's no one else in the world like you. And if and when *you* become a role model, beware of young admirers who try too hard to emulate you. In truth, there is no ideal management style and no ultimate role model. Life is enriched by diversity and diminished by sameness.

Compare, for example, Presidents George Washington and Abraham Lincoln. Could they have been less alike? Or Army Generals Omar Bradley and Norman Schwarzkopf. Or two successive CEOs of any first-rate company. How are they alike and how do they differ? And just how much of their leadership success derived from their styles? How much from their substance?

The Secret of Style: Substance

The empty-suited assistant described earlier lacked substance. Waiting to see what his mentor thought, casting his opinions in the direction of the prevailing winds, he could add no value to a discussion. The few ideas he expressed were not his own. He not only didn't have the "right stuff," he didn't seem to have any

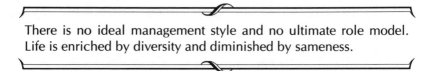

There is no ideal management style and no ultimate role model. Life is enriched by diversity and diminished by sameness.

stuff. In assessing your people, consider the stuff they're made of. What is the reality that underlies their outward appearance? And what is *your* reality?

This is not to say that style is worthless, if by style we mean a way of acting with ease of manner and in a way that makes others comfortable with us. A naturalness of action is worth cultivating, as is the ability to accept triumphs and disappointments with grace. Style in this sense has much to do with personality and even more to do with character. Character in turn derives largely from unimpaired integrity and from a sound set of values.

Given enough responsibilities and time, managers who remain true to their values develop into authentic leaders. The development of an authentic self (and hence of your unique "style") comes through achievement, through doing your homework, but also through failure, disappointment, persistence. Outward manifestations of style can be acquired quickly. But in business, as in sports, style is about performance, not appearance. Robert Fierle, founder and chairman of American Precision Industries, says you can look great on the golf course, but the question is whether you can put the ball in the cup.

The word "style" applies to consistent patterns of behavior. Erratic behavior creates confusion and blocks results. Threatening behavior thwarts open communication and impairs risk taking. Arrogant behavior demotivates those who deserve the credit. Overly serious behavior takes the fun out of work. This manner of behaving, or that, stems from beliefs, values, and attitudes. The "correct" style (if there is such a thing) is therefore one that is based on *your* beliefs, *your* values, *your* attitudes, and *your* convictions.

Management Styles From A to Z

There are many different CEO styles. Some CEOs (like Alcoa's Paul O'Neill and Quantum Chemical's John Hoyt Stookey) are cultured intellectuals. Others (Henry Ford and Soichiro Honda come quickly to mind) are rough-hewn and narrowly focused. Some, like Pfizer's Ed Pratt and AT&T's Robert Allen, are modest and approachable. Others, like Pan Am's former CEO Juan T. Trippe and IBM's former chairman T. Vincent Learson, came across as fearsome. One former Pan Am executive described Trippe as being "like Stalin. He knocked off everyone around him." In contrast, Herbert Kelleher, of Southwest Airlines, has been known to impersonate Elvis Presley and the Easter Bunny and to sing rap music accompanied by people dressed as tomatoes and Teenage Mutant Ninja Turtles.

Some stick to their knitting and spend little time seeking the limelight, while others seek the full spotlight. For example, in the mid-1980s, Hicks Waldron, then chairman and CEO of Avon, permitted business journalist Sonny Kleinfield to follow him around for months for the purpose of producing a book that would describe the life of a chief executive. "Watching Waldron sit through a parade of meetings," Kleinfield wrote, "it becomes apparent that a CEO inevitably finds his field of vision narrowed to a small world. Waldron's mind is an encyclopedia of sales figures for Campaign Ten, margins for Avon's skin-care products, print runs for the James River Traders catalogue, but there is never time to keep up with all else that goes on in the world which doesn't have a direct impact on Avon."

Waldron's response to this was that as a CEO "you become one of those people who knows more and more about less and less until you know everything about nothing." Kleinfield's chronicle of Waldron's pedestrian approaches and banal utterings confirms this.

Some publicity seekers, like Lee Iacocca and Donald Trump, take the more direct route of writing (with help) self-aggrandizing books. And a few CEOs, such as Ross Perot, founder and former CEO of Electronic Data Systems, and William Farley (before he lost control in 1991 of West Point-Pepperell, Inc.), seemed at times to be positioning themselves for a run at the U.S. presidency. Indeed, in 1992, Perot dramatically confirmed this.

Public persons or private, loose cannons or reflective thinkers, autocrats or participative leaders, CEOs come in every conceivable style. Some are better than others, but none is perfect. Yet with all their faults (and there are many), none could improve his or her effectiveness by trying to fit into the style of another. The song "I've Gotta Be Me" applies equally to CEOs and to managers at every organizational level beneath them.

What Really Counts

Your style as a manager ultimately depends on what you consider appropriate. And because of this, it's quite possible that you'll exhibit some variety of styles at different times in your career.

If you are charged with rescuing a failing company, for example, you'll make more decisions on your own and will make them faster. When you are new on a job, you'll probably consult more widely before making important decisions than when you've been in a management assignment for several years. But some things should never change.

At every point in your career there must be consistency between your words and your actions. There must be reasonable explanations for your actions and a willingness to share those explanations. And there must be growth and self-development all along the way.

The other elements of *how* you do your job are up to you. But by drawing strength from your inner self, you'll be developing your own style, and if you do this right, the mark you leave will be indelible.

Still, it is not only *how* you achieve this mark that counts. In the end, it is *what* you do that counts. And there is still another question—the inevitable question of *why*. What is the meaning of your efforts and accomplishments?

Many years ago, former Secretary of Health, Education, and Welfare John W. Gardner concluded a speech with a short paragraph on the subject of meaning. Over fifteen years later that final paragraph returned to him in a poignant way. A man wrote to him saying that when his twenty-year-old daughter was killed in an automobile accident, she was carrying in her wallet that paragraph:

> Meaning is not something you stumble across, like the answer to a riddle or the prize in a treasure hunt. Meaning is something you build into your life. You build it out of your own past, out of your affections and loyalties, out of the experience of humankind as it is passed on to you, out of your own talent and understanding, out of things you believe in, out of the things and people you love, out of the values for which you are willing to sacrifice something. The ingredients are there. You are the only one who can put them together into that unique pattern that will be your life. Let it be a life that has dignity and meaning for you. If it does, then the particular balance of success or failure is of less account.

In the final analysis, styles fade—but meanings endure. So while it is important to have a style—*your* style, not mine, not your boss's, not anyone else's—it's far more important to find that meaning.

Chapter Fifteen

A Touch of Class:
How Others See You and
What You Can Do About It

The executive image. . . . Articles, books, seminars, consultants, indeed whole companies are dedicated to this. The how-to-look-and-act-like-a-corporate-winner industry offers lots of advice. Dress for success. Learn how to sit and stand. Master public speaking. Graduate from the power necktie to the power breakfast.

The trouble with this preoccupation with style is twofold. First, fashions change. More important, no veneer can mask true character. Style comes from within.

This is not to say that you should give no thought to the way you look and act. On the contrary, the higher you rise in management, the more important your presence and its effect on others become. To achieve that climb, lower-level managers must be conscious of the impact they make both within and outside the corporate walls.

Many managers get confused about this. Preferring style to substance, they seem to forget that it's still their track record that counts. Nevertheless, showing concern, *genuine* concern, for other people in ways appropriate to your position can lubricate that track. Whether you're on the way up, plateaued, or sitting in the topmost corner office, remember one thing: Other people, and how you regard them, is what style is all about.

As I've discussed this topic with managers from time to time, I've noted some surprise about this point. So let me repeat it: Acquiring and maintaining style (or, as less stylish people call it, "class") is not about you. It's about making other people comfortable with you. And helping them to become more comfortable with themselves. That's the minimal threshold. But you can go beyond this by helping to make people *happy* with you and with themselves.

The issue of making others feel comfortable around you, while no small matter, is often addressed by small but thoughtful gestures. For example, if at the end of a dinner you note your guest, who may be less privileged and knowledgeable than you, taking a sip from the finger bowl, then surely you'd unblinkingly

> Acquiring and maintaining style is not about you. It's about making other people comfortable with you.

follow suit. This example, incidentally, is not a fictional one. (Nor is drinking tepid water all that bad.) Managers who are gracious, caring, and giving are likely to have real style.

Possessing such qualities makes it easier to live with yourself as well as to interrelate with others. Jan Yager, who has studied and written about it, claims that proper business protocol "offers you another strategy for getting to the top and staying there." Though this may not be the most selfless motive for developing tasteful behavior, research confirms her conviction.

In a large-scale project commissioned by the American Management Association, behavioral scientists identified something they called "concern with impact" as one of eighteen basic competencies (along with others such as logical thinking, conceptualization, and persuasiveness) that distinguish successful managers from the mediocre.

Concern with impact is the felt need to influence and persuade others and to uphold your and your organization's image and reputation. Those who possess such concern go far beyond standard courtesies.

Corny as it may sound, here's the formula for business courtesy: Follow the Golden Rule. And if you want to set yourself apart from others, upgrade your actions a notch or two by doing unto others what you *wish*—but could hardly expect—others to do for you.

Take the mundane issue of coffee in the office. Most managers, including most CEOs, chat with their guests while their assistants (a.k.a. gofers, formerly called "girls") head for the coffeepot. But John Diebold, chairman of the New York-based Diebold Group, personally pours and serves. Increasingly, so do many other chiefs. It's a small gesture, requiring little effort. Diebold even has a British tea-cozy-covered pot of hot water and a selection of teas. How could anyone fail to be impressed by this?

Fashion Notes for CEOs: Dress Down

Despite admonitions to the contrary, we tend to judge a book by its cover and to make quick and lasting judgments about people by their appearance. Clothes may not make the man or the woman, but they do make a statement that is hard to erase. A suit or dress of inappropriate style or color, an ill-groomed head of hair, a too vivid scarf or necktie, scuffed shoes—any one of these or dozens of other wrong choices—can handicap a manager's progress.

But what *is* wrong? In most business settings, anything that calls attention to itself. Different people have different levels of sensitivity regarding others' perceptions of them. For example, I squirm if a colleague compliments me on a necktie or notes a fresh haircut. You needn't be that hyper, but remember that style has to do with others' perceptions, not yours. The mirror exists to let you see yourself as they do.

The most tasteful executives I know dress, and act, in an understated way. What is understated or overstated depends to some degree on your work environment. Companies and industries vary greatly in what is considered appropriate work apparel. Ultimately, however, understatedness or overstatedness is in the eye of the beholder.

As you climb the organizational ladder, you'll probably want your apparel to be increasingly conservative. According to business writer James P. Sterba:

> To become a chief executive, you have to get dull in stages, shedding just enough humanity, whimsy, col-

legiality and sartorial eccentricity with each promotion to exhibit a bit more of the progress, maturation and fine-tuning required to comfort (or sedate) board members and shareholders. As a fast-rising underling, you want to excite. As CEO you want to soothe.

He describes this "reverse metamorphosis" from butterfly to worm as a delicate maneuver, and for emphasis he quotes Dave Barry, author of *Claw Your Way to the Top*: "Basically, the American businessman should dress as though he recently lost his entire family in a tragic boat explosion." Then Sterba advises us to buy only silk. And, for that matter, "never wear any clothes made out of petroleum, only fibers made by sheep, plants or worms."

Beneath that whimsy there's a germ of truth, but only a germ. In real life, CEOs cannot let themselves become dull. And as they rise to that position, they must increase, rather than shed, their humanity, collegiality, and sense of humor.

Nor should they *look* dull. Or at least not exactly dull. Still,

> "The American businessman should dress as though he recently lost his entire family in a tragic boat explosion."

successful chief executives, both men and women, tend to dress in a quietly tasteful, rather than flamboyant, way. For women, this does not imply a mannish corporate uniform. When Cathleen Black was publisher of *USA Today*, she made this comment: "I think it's ridiculous to try to be a man in a pinstriped suit" and said that she wore "about the same kind of things I always wore." A visiting niece who was a middle manager at Sprint once admired a red Chanel-like dress Black was wearing at home. "She said she loved my dress, but that she could never wear it to work. I had just worn it to the office that day!" Both were probably right.

Your Office: Room With a View—Of You

Remember that your work attire tells something about you but more importantly sends a message about how you regard those with whom you come in contact. The same is true of your office decor.

In most companies, on the way up you can begin to let your office make more of a statement than at earlier times. But until you've reached the top, that statement should resonate in harmony with the culture of your organization and should be appropriate to your level within it.

At some companies, notably Hewlett-Packard and Texas Instruments, even the offices of the chiefs have historically been modest, perhaps because their corporate memories recall their modest beginnings. At others, especially in industries such as advertising and entertainment, when it comes to posh, the sky's no limit. A tasteful office, however, does not need to strain the corporate budget.

Applying the principle of form follows function, ask yourself about the purposes you wish your office to serve. In my case I've preferred in recent years to have a welcoming round table and comfortable chairs in the center of the room and a stand-up desk elsewhere for my personal use. This has made for reasonably clutter-free, sociable meetings. An even better plan, if affordable, is to have an adjoining small back office, which can be as messy as you'd like.

When it comes to decor, chief executives' offices run the gamut. Frank Pace, former CEO of General Dynamics and Secretary of the Army, lined his International Executive Service Corps office with photographs and mementos of dozens of world statesmen. Curiously, this did not seem ostentatious, though for most people it would have. Pace would escort first-time visitors cordially down memory lane as he recounted one interesting anecdote after another. Somehow Pace made this a wholly charming experience. At the other extreme I've seen some offices that are starkly modern, almost bare, yet still welcoming.

In sharp contrast, Admiral Hyman Rickover, responsible for building nuclear submarines during the 1950s, seemed more interested in making his guests unwelcome. He sat behind a mammoth desk on a raised chair, while his visitor had only the option of sitting in an uncomfortable straight chair whose front legs had been shortened—and with a glaring desk lamp all but blinding him. Not world-famous for his hospitality, Rickover nevertheless designed a functional office. Its purpose was to serve the diminutive admiral as a sort of inquisition chamber in which he could pressure vendors, congressional aides, and others of that ilk. And he made his point graphically.

Your image as a manager has to do with much more than visual impact, however. You're constantly being judged by what you say and how you say it. A well-modulated voice is a great asset. How you use that voice and what you say is even more important. An educated vocabulary is very important. This includes telephone courtesy, which is no trivial matter. Letitia Baldrige, internationally recognized for her expertise on etiquette, has listed forty-four personal qualities displayed by good managers that "make life at work more liveable for everyone." And she's listed twenty good and bad qualities of voice suitable for executive stature, and hundreds of useful rules and suggestions, helpful to managers as they navigate among the manifold Scyllae and Charybdes of their careers.

The central question should be this: What is appropriate? Appropriate from the others' point of view? What will make people most comfortable? What will please them?

Surprisingly, many will be pleased just by your knowing their names and how to pronounce them. That's a simple enough thing to learn. And people you haven't seen for a while will be pleased by your quickly giving your own name. In the American culture, a warm smile and friendly handshake are appropriate. People in foreign lands will be pleased if you take the time to learn something about their cultures. Maybe they don't want to be touched or grinned at.

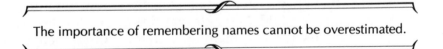

The importance of remembering names cannot be overestimated.

People listening to you speak are pleased whenever you have prepared your comments and tailored them to suit the audience. Incidentally, I have found that when speaking to a foreign audience through an interpreter, two things are important. First, get a very good interpreter. And, second, spend some time with that interpreter. By doing this, some of my overseas speeches have enjoyed remarkably good reception—not nearly so much for what

I've said as for the quality of what they've heard, through another's voice.

In any country the importance of remembering names cannot be overestimated. As a senior executive you should learn the names of as many people in your organization as possible. The personal touch in brief, passing conversations is as important to them as to your directors.

If you should find yourself hosting a group of, say, fifty people at a reception, it's not impossible to circulate widely enough to talk for a few minutes with each. An approach I use is to scan the guest list ahead of time, thinking of matters that might be of interest to those I know (and asking about those I don't). Then after the affair I review it again to see who, if anyone, I missed. My standard is 100 percent. If you adopt this standard but sometimes fail to reach it, a follow-up phone call will at least let them know you cared enough to acknowledge them.

Controlling Those Twittering Hormones

Finally, there is the matter of dealing with members of the opposite sex. Surely by now most managers must know what is considered sexist or inappropriate, but many still seem either not to know or not to care. If you're still in this category, give the issue about five minutes of serious thought, again from the other person's point of view. If even after doing this, your hormones start twittering at the sight of that luscious blond, or gorgeous hunk, down the hall, try to control yourself. Try to imagine that this is your sibling, though perhaps a younger one—your own flesh-and-blood sibling for God's sake. If that doesn't work, then join Sexists Anonymous. Or do something. Anything other than what your animal instincts are urging you to do.

But what about consenting adults? you ask. Remember, we're talking about your career here, not your love life. And it's just possible that what looks to you like a sexy come-on may be just a friendly smile. The upward journey from a salesperson's territory or engineer's bench to the CEO position is long and tortuous. A sexual harassment suit along the way would be less than helpful.

Instead of hitting on that object of your potential affection, you might consider holding out a helping hand. Inexperienced managers could benefit from your experience, and a mentoring relationship with younger people could help your organization as well as them. Mentoring yields a selfish benefit, too. Because the best way to learn any subject is to teach it, and because prepara-

> Do something. Anything other than what your animal instincts are urging you to do.

tion for mentoring sessions requires reflection, this might help improve your performance too. And your perspective.

Even if your thoughts are on the right plane, thoughtless actions in this modern day of attractive women and men mingling in the workplace can trigger problems. For example, a newly appointed executive assistant to the chairman of a Fortune 100 company needed to reach a senior executive late one night. Finding he had just left for the airport, she left this message with his wife, without further explanation: "Just tell him Chrissie called, and I'll catch up with him on the road." The young assistant had completely failed to think about her message from anyone's standpoint other than her own.

Managers who consistently look at their world through others' eyes, and habitually help other people, inevitably develop an admirable style. A genuine style. It is such managers who become authentic leaders.

Chapter Sixteen

The Energizing Power of Passion

The most productive and impressive people I know are passionate about the work they do. The best actors are in love with their craft. Accomplished cabinetmakers admire wood and virtually caress their tools as they work. Good writers become excited whenever they find just the right word or turn of phrase. This passion for their work shines through in the finished product, whether it be a polished stage performance, a piece of fine furniture, or a gripping novel.

This is no less true of the best CEOs. They embrace their work with passion. But there is one difference. Unlike artists and craftsmen, chief executives are accountable for the results of others. Many others. It is therefore not enough to be passionate about your own contributions. It is not even enough to be enthusiastic about your customers and your products. That feeling must embrace your people as well, and what they do.

Sigmund Freud described our two basic needs. Love and work, he said. He did not say we need to love our work. But the best workers do, whether they are blue-collar or white-collar, whether clerical, professional, or managerial. And certainly the best CEOs do. The particular work of a CEO is to provide leadership, but who among the best leaders considers that work? Still, leadership is something of an abstract concept. So the question is this: Do you love whatever it is that you and your people do? Are you passionate about their work?

Ken Iverson, chairman and CEO of the Nucor Corporation, is a metallurgist by training. But he considers himself a "hot metal man." He likes molten steel. "Hot metal has a fascination all its own," he says. "There is a fascination about melting metal and pouring it into a shape. A hot metal man has to feel that fascination. That's why he works around hot metal." But Iverson is also committed to his people, and that's why they like to work around him.

Anthony O'Reilly, CEO of H. J. Heinz, brought to his company a sharply redefined marketing focus. "One of the reasons why I am often identified with marketing," he says, "is that I am very responsive to demographic changes and I am fascinated by media changes in the world." But O'Reilly is also fascinated by people, and especially their behavior.

Joichi Aoi, chief executive of Toshiba, says, "You have to identify yourself with a piece of work and stand for that work. We talk about the wealth of work. That is an end in itself."

Other successful CEOs, like Richard F. Teerlink of Harley-Davidson, may be passionate about the products their people turn out (in his case, motorcycles). Or, like Scandinavian Airlines Sys-

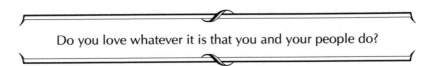

Do you love whatever it is that you and your people do?

tem CEO Jan Carlzon or Stew Leonard, founder of the famous Dairy Store, they may be passionate about helping their people to make customers so pleased that they'll convey their enthusiasm to others. Whatever it is, molten metal, motorcycles, or marketing, the passion must be there. Not just for the products and processes, but for your people.

Interestingly, O'Reilly does not consider Heinz's core competency to be marketing, despite its impressive marketing talents. Nor does he consider it to be the company's skills in food production, packaging, or distribution. Instead, when asked about his company's core competency, he says, "Professional collegiality is something we prize greatly. By that I mean a form of community within the organization that promotes support, openness, and candor and is underwritten by our structured goal setting, compensation, and the sense of ownership that all the senior executives have."

In other words, like other first-rate CEOs, O'Reilly is passionate about the way his people work together in common cause. Indeed, he's a leader *because* he's passionate about the leadership his whole team brings to the enterprise, not just his own personal contribution.

Sparking the Organization

Excitement is contagious. By allowing your emotions to be observed, you are giving permission to your people to let their feelings be shown, their fervor, their commitment. When these emotions work their way through the organization, the whole work force becomes energized. There is electricity in the air all over the place. Pride develops. And that becomes contagious too.

As you celebrate your people's achievements with them, and together commit yourselves to greater ones, there is nothing that can substitute for the emotional, even spiritual, component of that commitment. Your optimism, your zeal, the fire of your feelings spark others. No intellectual presentations, no matter how well reasoned, and no flowery rhetoric that lacks genuine ardor can do the job. Once you capture the hearts of your people, their minds will follow. That simply doesn't work the other way around.

As CEO, it's your job to energize your organization and to keep it energized. There's been much talk in recent years about the role of chief executive as cheerleader. Some of this is needed, especially when you're losing the game. At such times you need

> Once you capture the hearts of your people, their minds will follow.

to remind your people of past successes and to convince them that future challenges can be surmounted just as past challenges were.

But most of the time CEOs should be fully engaged as team players, not just as people standing on the sidelines exhorting the team. Indeed energy is transmitted not by exhortation but by example. And it is results that deserve celebration, not just efforts, no matter how heroic. Nevertheless, efforts, especially against great odds, must be encouraged. Again, the chief executive must lead the way.

Being Bullheaded About Brick Walls

Most chief executives I know seem to have inexhaustible energy, and when they come up against a brick wall, they simply keep going. They show endless tenacity and are persistent to a fault. Still, sometimes what is needed is not more bullheadedness but a completely fresh look. At such times it's important to stand back, to step aside to gain perspective and decide whether you need to rechannel your energies. Misplaced passion won't help. You may need to focus your attention on the task of finding a new direction. At such times, enthusiasm alone can't do the job.

It's important to remember that despite your apparently bottomless resource of psychic energy, there is really a bottom to it. So remember to take care of yourself. For there are some contributions to your organization that only you can make.

Earlier, we talked about your unique responsibility for your company's future, something that cannot be delegated. You also have the responsibility to furnish or acquire fresh intellectual capital and to create the kind of receptivity to new ideas that is needed to spark innovation and change. Additionally, you have certain powers that others do not have—the power, for example, to reshape the organization's culture. And you have the power, whether or not you recognize it, to manage others' attention and focus.

If, for example, you look only—or consistently first—at financial results, so will your people, at all levels. But if you focus instead on quality of product or customer service, or growth, or new markets, or innovation, your people will follow your lead. For that reason, if no other, one of the most important things to think about is your agenda as CEO. Just where should the energies of your people be directed?

Your agenda, of course, will be where your passion lies. If you are emotionally attuned to your customers, your agenda (your real agenda, whether written or unwritten) will be to serve them. If you're passionate about cutting costs, as some CEOs certainly are, then cost cutting will be near the top of your priority list. You might ask yourself: What has been my agenda so far?

After having been in the CEO's position for a few years, you'll begin to notice changes that have come about, changes that *you* have brought about, whether consciously or not. Are these changes the kinds of changes you had hoped for, or planned? You'll be leaving a mark on your organization and have a limited time to make that mark. What would you like your successor to say about you in the first annual letter to shareholders after your retirement? What will your legacy be?

Many chief executives preside rather than lead. Such agents of the status quo, when they depart, inevitably leave their organizations weaker than when they arrived. For in organizational life, as in your personal life, there *is* no status quo. Change-agent chiefs leave organizations that are markedly different from the way they were when they entered. Some companies have been greatly strengthened, others badly wounded. Some strong chief executives with long tenures, like Armand Hammer of Occidental Petroleum, leave marks so distinctive that their successors spend early energies in trying to erase them. What is *your* mark, or what will it be?

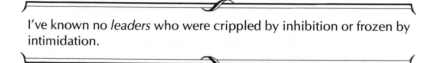

I've known no *leaders* who were crippled by inhibition or frozen by intimidation.

During the middle period of your tenure as chief, it's time to take stock. And maybe to make some midcourse corrections. Is your agenda the right one? Is it clear, simple to understand? Does it conform to those things you feel most convinced, most passionate about? Most important, are those one or two major goals that are so important to you equally important to the future of your organization, or could they be ego-driven? As important as passion is, it must be tempered by objectivity. And your goals must be tested by reality.

Still, if in your tenure so far you've been a leader, with all that this implies, your ideas *have* been tested by the inherent reality of what your people think. If you've been open and above-board, then your agenda has been set not by you alone but by the leadership support group you've assembled—the people who've later helped you accomplish your agenda, or at least to make a dent in it. You've had idea-clashing exchanges and exhaustive debates, and you've all learned from each other. Your agenda has been forged, like hot metal, by the fires of your enthusiasm, and theirs.

Maybe there is some other way to lead, some way to lead without passion. If so, I've never witnessed it. I have known some *managers* who are so inhibited by self-consciousness that they cannot express themselves freely and with emotion. And I've known quite a few who were intimidated to speak out for fear of embarrassment. But I've known no *leaders* who were crippled by inhibition or frozen by intimidation. So we end up where we started out. What are *you* passionate about?

What Makes You Weep?

Max DePree, chairman and former CEO of Herman Miller, the furniture manufacturer that was named by *Fortune* magazine as one of the ten best-managed and innovative U.S. companies, left as part of his legacy a small book, almost a poem, called *Leadership Is an Art*. Toward its end, he asks whether grown men weep and whether they should. His answer to both questions: Of course. And he says that anyone in touch with reality knows there are many reasons to weep. Then he suggests that there are some things we probably ought to weep about. On his list he includes, among others, these: superficiality, arrogance, looking at customers as interruptions, and leaders who watch bottom lines without watching behavior. And he adds, too, some things we should weep about for joy: great news, tenderness, and a word of thanks, for example.

I believe we should weep in sadness for those who try to lead without being fully themselves. We should weep whenever we see CEOs acting as though they care more for themselves than for their people. We should weep for joy when leadership begins to blossom at the lowest levels of our organization. And we should weep most of all, in pain, whenever such budding leadership is thwarted.

The question, though, is not what it would take to bring a tear to the eye of Max DePree, or mine. The question is what it takes to make *you* weep. What are *your* passions? And how do they fit into your leadership behavior as chief executive?

Think about this, too: When you step down as CEO, will others weep? Remember that there are tears of joy and tears of pain. Which kind of tears will your people shed as you depart? Or, will your lack of passion, your lack of emotional connection to them, make your farewell ceremony just another retirement party? If so, I weep for you.

Chapter Seventeen

Passing the Torch— But to Whom?

As the Cold War melted down, aficionados of spy novels expressed serious concern. What could possibly replace the cloak-and-dagger accounts of John le Carré and Robert Ludlum about the skullduggery between the CIA and the KGB? Not to worry. There's more than enough intrigue in the executive suite during the CEO succession process to satisfy the most voracious appetite for tales of hugger-mugger.

As a chief executive approaches retirement age, posturing and politicking go into high gear. Potential candidates for succession begin undercover promotional campaigns, subtly marketing themselves as best they can. In publicly held companies, boards have had the opportunity to get to know, at least to a limited extent, the inside directors. Now they may notice them jockeying for a position on the inside track.

Meanwhile, hundreds of observers join those who consider themselves contenders in looking for signals. Who is the CEO spending the most time with these days? Especially behind closed doors. Who is traveling with the CEO? What do recent shifts in responsibility mean? Unless this speculation is contained, the distraction it causes can have a devastating effect on the business. And if no succession plan is in place, this speculation simply can't be controlled.

Some chief executives postpone any thought about succession until the very last minute. Indeed some, thinking themselves immortal, give little or no thought to succession, as they're incapable of conceiving that there will *be* a last minute.

Juan T. Trippe, who in the early 1930s helped found the airline that became Pan Am, abruptly resigned his chairmanship in 1968. At Trippe's recommendation, Pan Am's board chose as chairman and CEO then-president Harold Gray (who was known by Trippe to be dying of cancer) and, as Gray's successor as president, attorney Najeeb Halaby—whom Trippe had recruited from his post as Federal Aviation Administrator only three years earlier. Predictably, Gray soon retired for health reasons, and in 1969, Halaby became chief. Perhaps just as predictably, given his lack of operating experience and Pan Am's troubled condition, its board forced Halaby's resignation in 1972.

Meanwhile, Trippe continued to roam the forty-sixth floor of the Pan Am Building, perhaps waiting to be called back to active duty. After all, he had been called back once before, some thirty years earlier. In 1939, Trippe's board of directors had orchestrated a coup, retaining Trippe as president and general manager but replacing him as chairman and CEO with Cornelius Vanderbilt Whitney. By failing to cooperate with Whitney and by demanding other executives' loyalty, Trippe had managed to sandbag Whitney and outwit his board. As a result, he was returned to the top position in 1940.

But history was not to repeat itself. Trippe would never return to the cockpit again. Instead, to succeed Halaby, William T. Seawell, president of Rolls-Royce and former head of operations for American Airlines, was picked to pilot Pan Am. Despite his and others' best efforts, the airline continued to lose altitude, year by year.

Almost two decades later, after a bankruptcy judge endorsed a plan calling for the removal of then-CEO Thomas G. Plaskett, Pan Am's board in 1991 chose Russell L. Ray, Jr., to lead the shrunken airline, which by then was concentrating on flying down to Rio and the Caribbean, just as its fabled Clippers had done so many years before. But the glamour was gone. And Juan Trippe was no longer around to witness the end of the story. Later that year, despite bankruptcy protection and a $115 million lift from Delta, Pan Am ran out of gas and shut itself down— leaving romantic memories and thousands of stranded passengers and employees.

At least Trippe took the step of retirement. Some other CEO immortals do not. Armand Hammer, who purchased Occidental

Petroleum Corporation in 1956, stayed on as chief executive until his death in 1990 at age 92. According to reports, Hammer had chosen a posthumous successor in the person of Ray R. Irani, who almost immediately went to work de-Hammerizing Occidental by cutting its dividend, selling its assets, and dealing with the various organizational and financial debris left by his predecessor's thirty-four-year reign. The annual report published just months after Hammer's death carried no picture of him.

The tortured sagas of Pan Am and Occidental dramatically illustrate that even the legacies of such long-running CEOs as Trippe and Hammer fade. So there's no point in seeking perpetuity for your reputation as a great CEO. Instead, a wiser course would be to seek a successor capable of perpetuating the *company*.

There has been all sorts of good advice about succession planning. The trouble is, to be succeeded you must first retire. This means giving up your job, your power, your CEO-level in-

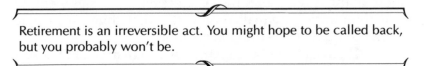

Retirement is an irreversible act. You might hope to be called back, but you probably won't be.

come and trappings, and, in many cases, even your identity. On the other hand, saying goodbye to all of this can be a sweet experience. You'll be told how much you'll be missed and how much you've done and meant to so many people. Never before your retirement dinner will you have heard such splendid testimonials to your character and capability.

The problem is, for most CEOs retirement is an irreversible act. You might *hope* to be called back, but you probably won't be. Emily Dickinson wasn't thinking of CEOs approaching the end of their careers when she wrote "Parting is all we know of heaven, and all we need of hell." But her words apply.

Are You Ready for the Inevitable?

Remember back to your first day as CEO? Remember how you did not feel different but found that you *were* different? Get ready: Now you're about to become different again. All that attention that is focused on you, attention you've come to believe you deserve, will be channelled to your successor. But look at the bright side of things. At least you'll get to know who your true friends are.

Still, who wants to rush toward that moment of truth? After all, as CEO you know more about the job than your successor possibly can, so maybe just one more year. Or two or three. You're healthy, you love your job, and from every indication your people love you. As well they should. And then there's the irrefutable logic that *you* are a known quantity. No matter how you slice it, selecting a successor is a roll of the dice.

Nevertheless, the time will come (and maybe it is already here) when you'll have to step down. Long before you do, you should have identified at least one, and preferably more, successor candidates. In 1953, Ralph J. Cordiner, then president of General Electric, said this: "The chief executive officer, if he is discharging his responsibility . . . should, within a period of not longer than three years after he has accepted his assignment, have at least three officers equal to or better than himself in performance who could succeed to his position."

In 1981, James D. Robinson 3rd, chairman and CEO of American Express, thought the matter equally important but perhaps not so urgent, when he said, "In my opinion, your primary job as chief executive is to build a management team that can do the job better tomorrow than you are doing it today. And if you haven't managed to do that in ten years or so, you've failed to do your job."

Circumstances can arrive, however, that require immediate succession long before the ten-year, or even three-year, period is up. Contingencies must be planned for, especially at the top. In my view, even the newest CEO must have in mind one or more potential successors. In a publicly held company, those names should be shared with your directors. As time goes on, and as you become more knowledgeable about the performance and potential of your people, the matter of succession should be continuously revisited. And because unforeseen circumstances do arrive, it's important to have more than one candidate in mind.

At American Express, Robinson followed his own advice. By 1987, ten years after having been elected chairman and CEO, he had an outstanding candidate on board in the person of Louis V. Gerstner, Jr., then president of the organization. But in 1989,

Gerstner left American Express to become chairman and CEO of RJR Nabisco. Two years later, Harvey Golub was named president. Still, Robinson said that Golub's promotion was not a succession plan. By that time, Robinson had been CEO for fourteen years. It had taken over two years to replace Gerstner as president and, if Robinson's public statement was true, it appeared that a revised succession plan was still to be worked out. Barely three months later, Golub took on an additional assignment, when Edwin M. Cooperman, chairman and co-CEO of its Travel Related Services Company, left American Express to join Primerica. Meanwhile, the parent company was facing difficult times. At the time Golub was made president, Robinson was still, at age 55, relatively young. However, many who knew him well doubted that he'd remain chairman for another ten years. Asked what would happen if Robinson were to decide to leave sooner, Golub said, "Then the board will make a decision."

The board is the ultimate decision maker, but it is you as CEO who must guide its members. The first step is to let them know your intended retirement date. As Lee Iacocca approached age 65, there was much speculation within the automotive industry about his retirement plans and Chrysler's succession plans. Finally, in late 1991, at age 66, he announced his plan to retire in 1992. Chrysler president Robert Lutz, then 59, was generally considered as Iacocca's logical successor. But the Chrysler chairman remained uncharacteristically silent. Before Lutz, there had been other logical successors—Gerald Greenwald, for example, former Chrysler vice-chairman, who had left to head up United Airlines.

By early 1992, the intrigue at Chrysler had thickened. Reports surfaced that its board, a year earlier, had planned to name former racing car driver Roger Penske as chief. But Penske, so the story went, had declined—not being prepared to wait indefinitely for Iacocca to leave the track. Who, then, would be selected? Vice-Chairman R. S. "Steve" Miller seemed next in line, but suddenly he left Chrysler to become an investment banker, thus aborting still another possible succession plan. Lutz again seemed the likely candidate. But wait! The UAL employee buy-out plan, for which Greenwald had left Chrysler, had also aborted. Now with Dillon, Read & Co., Greenwald was said to be chatting with Iacocca, by then age 67. Chrysler's directors were reported to be getting a bit edgy, and for good reason. So, no doubt, was Robert Lutz.

Meanwhile, at IBM, some of *its* most talented senior people were walking out the door. George H. Conrades, long widely thought to be the logical successor to CEO John F. Akers—and described by one consultant as the most sought-after executive in the United States—had been demoted, in late 1991. So, a few months later, he took early retirement to devote full-time efforts to evaluating job offers. Only a week earlier, C. Michael Armstrong, head of IBM's enormous foreign sales operation, had quit to run Hughes Aircraft, having been told by Akers that he was not in the running. Other officers left as well. Only three years short of age 60 (IBM's normal retirement age for senior officers), Akers was apparently looking toward a younger—and hence less seasoned—pool of talent as possible succession material. Or so went the rumors at the battered and bruised Big Blue. Some speculated otherwise: that Akers was beginning to have second thoughts about IBM's age-60 retirement tradition.

In March 1992, Chrysler's directors held a rare Saturday meeting, lasting until midnight, at which they named GM's Robert J. Eaton vice-chairman and chief operating officer—and successor to Lee Iacocca upon his retirement as CEO at the end of the year.

Staying too long at the fair may damage your organization. Remember, those who are competent enough to succeed you are also competent enough to lead other organizations. And they simply may become impatient, especially if you delay your plans.

In early 1991, Richard P. Banis, president and chief operating officer of Circus Enterprises, the Las Vegas casino company, was identified as its next chairman and CEO. It was understood that he would take office within a year when William G. Bennett retired as CEO. But a few months later, Bennett decided that projects scheduled over the next few years were just too exciting for him to leave, so he decided to postpone his retirement. Banis, then 46, suddenly resigned in view of Bennett's change of heart and the uncertainty over his retirement plans.

There are lots of reasons you can find to postpone retirement. Maybe you think there's no one good enough to replace you. Harry Gray, former chairman and CEO of United Technologies, started looking in 1975 but simply couldn't find the right successor. Edward Hennessey, Jr., disappointed him. According to Gray, Hennessey was lobbying with board members for him to

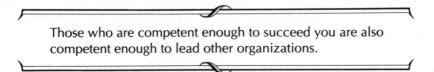

Those who are competent enough to succeed you are also competent enough to lead other organizations.

retire. Alexander Haig became U.S. Secretary of State. Peter Scott resigned to seek a different life-style. Robert Carlson's business judgment seemed so flawed to Gray that he fired him. Soon after that, Gray selected Robert Daniell as president, after which the UT board (which had seen a parade of possible successors come and go) began insisting that Gray step down. Finally, in 1986, two years after Daniell's assumption of the presidency, Gray did relinquish his chief executive post—but he still clung to his chairmanship. "My problem," he later explained, "is that I'm a lousy picker."

Failing to plan for succession can be risky, not just for your organization, but for you as CEO. In 1990, the Allied-Signal board noticed that its sixty-three-year-old chairman and CEO Edward Hennessey, Jr., (that's right, the same Hennessey who much earlier had been passed over at UT) had not groomed a successor from within. So they called in an executive search firm to begin the long process of seeking a suitable outside candidate. As a result of the search, General Electric vice-chairman Lawrence A. Bossidy was recommended. Hennessey, who had planned to remain in the job for another year or two, saw his retirement plans radically changed when Bossidy indicated an understandable unwillingness to wait that long. "We learned," said Hennessey, "that the better the guy was, the sooner he wanted to become CEO." (An *amazing* revelation!)

Insiders vs. Outsiders

In well-run organizations, after the CEO has served for a few years, there should be several potential successors from within. We've talked about delegation and teamwork, the development of people, and leadership support. We've talked about the importance of CEOs' surrounding themselves with people better than they are in their particular fields. And because the CEO has no responsibility more important to the organization's future than the task of selecting and grooming a successor, there should be no need to look outside the organization.

Yet boards of directors are increasingly doing just this. In recent years, outsiders have represented more than one-fourth of all newly hired chief executives. Just as Allied-Signal's current CEO came from General Electric, Campbell Soup's came from Gerber Products. Alcoa's from International Paper. Goodyear's from Rubbermaid. Gulfstream Aerospace's from Xerox. Tenneco's from Union Pacific. Laura Ashley's from Thorn EMI (a consumer electronics and appliance rental business). Hughes Aircraft's from IBM. Many of these outside appointments represented moves across industry lines. And each time a board elected an outsider, even from the same industry, it took a significant risk. This is confirmed by a recent study by A. T. Kearney, the management consultant firm, which found that twelve out of thirteen of the CEOs of the most profitable Fortune 200 firms over the period from 1970 to 1988 had been promoted from within.

Some boards of directors have been getting lots of practice in naming CEOs. And some have been getting too much practice. For example, Robert R. Ferguson 3rd (an insider) became, in 1991, the *ninth* chief executive of Continental Airlines over a *nine-year* period.

Even worse, some boards, when succession time comes, seem not only not to have a plan, they seem not to have a clue. This remarkable condition has helped give rise to the use of interim chief executives. John A. Thompson, chairman and founder of the Interim Management Corporation, a firm specializing in such placements, claims there are benefits in hiring non-permanent CEOs, particularly for turnaround situations. For one thing, they carry no emotional baggage pertaining to the firm. And he quotes one such interim CEO who was faced with turning around a national retail chain:

> As an outsider I bring certain advantages. I try to be dispassionate and analytical, and of course I am not shackled by the organization's history. . . . Turnarounds move much more quickly when you have someone who

is tuned in to rapid change, understands it, can articulate needs and educate the organization to execute solutions.

Granted, an interim CEO may be just the right ticket, especially in emergency situations when there is no other ticket to be had. But an emergency of this kind exists only because the matter of succession has not been properly attended to. The directors, or in the case of privately held companies, the owners, have simply failed to do their most important task. And the previous CEO has failed as well.

Not all such failures are sins of omission, for there are CEOs whose reluctance to retire is so strong that they sabotage the succession process—for example, by sponsoring a candidate whom the board is likely to resist or who, if chosen, is sure to fail. The history of CEO succession is replete with such examples. Most failures of succession at the top, however, come through neglect. The burdens of day-to-day responsibilities and *crises du jour* more than adequately fill the time available to CEOs. Still, because the future of your organization cannot be delegated, the inevitable transition must be planned for.

Putting Your Company's Future in the Right Hands

Just what *is* your responsibility for succession? And what steps should you take? First, realize that the end of your tenure will come. Try to grasp this fact emotionally, not just intellectually. And second, act upon that realization both early and throughout your career as CEO.

As you are building your initial top team, it's important to identify one or more team members who could take over with some success in an emergency. As time goes on, you'll get to know your people, their strengths and shortcomings. If none is an appropriate potential successor, then it's time to add to your team a couple of people who have such strengths. But what are your criteria? It's easy to develop an endless list that, as the saying goes, God on a good day could not meet. Still, you need criteria. The top two on my list are integrity and courage. (Given, of course, a high level of business experience and acumen.)

Succession planning is an iterative process and, when done well, requires considerable time. Those who in your private thoughts might qualify need to be given successively increasing challenges and responsibilities. The test, and fair assessment, of their successes and failures may take years. You'll need to observe both the long-term consequences of their decisions and the effects of their strategies.

It may be difficult for you alone to make these judgments. And the selection of a successor is too delicate, and often too political, to discuss except with your most trusted confidants. At some point, you'll need to share your thoughts with the board and to get them to share theirs, for the ultimate decision, and responsibility, will be theirs.

The best transitions are characterized by some degree of continuity. Your successor will make his or her mark and indeed may drastically change the organization's direction. Yet that person will need to build upon what you have done. Your successor's changes, however drastic they may be, will be more effective if leavened by continuity, if linked to what you've accomplished.

Yet it is a rare succession that does not bring some disruption. One purpose of succession planning is to minimize that disruption to avoid organizational loss of momentum in the market. But the main purpose is to ensure, to the extent you can, a successful future for the company you've been responsible for, and which you must eventually leave. Sadly, many chief executives who have otherwise led their organizations well fail miserably at this, their most important single task.

The best CEOs are those who consistently put the interests of their organizations above their own. When they retire, they depart with the knowledge that they've done their jobs completely, by having helped the organization put its future in the right hands. But there's nothing easy about handling succession.

It's one thing to find people better than you in their particular fields but quite another to identify, and be sure of, someone who'll be as good as you in the overall leadership post. Moreover, it's difficult to be objective. As CEO you have a well-developed ego. You had to have this to take the job. Chances are it's been developed even further on the job. And it's hard to judge impersonally someone with whom you've developed close relationships. Yet judge you must.

Chapter Eighteen

Moving On:
Is There Life
After Retirement?

Chief executives exit their careers in a variety of ways. Some need to be virtually pried off center stage and carried away, kicking and screaming, even though they've long ago lost their audience. Others, with much fanfare, make dramatic exits but wait in the wings to be called back for one last performance. Still others take their final bows and gracefully exit but hang around backstage for a while doing useful odd jobs, or devote themselves to representing the cast to the public. Finally, there are those who, when their final curtain comes down, simply say goodbye to the rest of the cast and walk straight out of the theater.

Former Harvard professor Jeffrey Sonnenfeld, now director for the Center for Leadership and Career Change at Emory University, having studied the retirement patterns of hundreds of chief executives, has categorized these departing CEOs, respectively, as monarchs, generals, ambassadors, and governors. His findings show that their styles of leaving office are correlated not with their management styles while on active duty but with their identification with heroic stature and their quest, in varying degrees, for immortal status.

To those who have not tasted the challenge and rewards of being a chief executive, the departure behavior of some CEOs may be hard to fathom. It is easy to understand why founders of companies might find leaving difficult, having put their whole lives into their enterprises. It's not difficult to understand the reluctance of the head of a family business to turn over the reins of leadership to a son or daughter or some other relative, with all the emotional baggage that such a power shift implies. But it may seem strange that among the "monarchs," those most adamant about staying on, are the numerous hired guns, chief executives who are merely corporate employees.

In 1984, as the directors of United Technologies continued to encourage Harry Gray to settle on a recommended successor, Gray went public by asking, "Who the blazes cares if it takes three months, thirteen months, or two years?" Obviously, it was his board of directors who cared, and as it turned out, it did take two more years.

Till Death Do Us Part?

Some tenacious CEOs literally prefer to face death rather than retirement. Charles Bluhdorn of Gulf & Western died at age 56 of a heart attack, having never recommended a successor to his board. Had he not died in this way, there would still have been good reason for him to confront succession, for as his directors later learned, for three years before his death Bluhdorn knew he had cancer. Bluhdorn's successor, Martin Davis, immediately went to work undoing much of what his predecessor had built. Had Bluhdorn lived longer, there is every indication that he would have clung to his office until the end, and by doing so he would simply have postponed the inevitable restructuring.

Chief executives who stay to the bitter end and must eventually be removed are those who see their work as their whole life's purpose. And they are not unlike people in other walks of life who identify themselves by what they do, not by who they are.

Such as an English professor at Clarion University of Pennsylvania named Terry Caesar who, in 1991, published an article in the *South Atlantic Quarterly* called "On Teaching at a Second-Rate University." The article began this way: "What is worth knowing? Teaching at a second-rate university is knowing, at least, that you're not worth knowing." The implication was that if you're teaching at a first-rate university, then you are really something, or at least somebody, rather than a nobody.

CEOs *know* that they are somebody, and those without a life outside their narrow, occupational definition of themselves simply perceive that the act of retirement will turn them into nobodies. So they postpone to the latest day possible their fall into the great abyss of nothingness.

This constricted self-image may also account for the behavior of those chiefs who ostensibly leave the stage but who both conspire behind the scenes with loyal board members to undercut their successors and express a willingness to return.

Adding to the behavior of those who are reluctant to retire or eager to return is the indisputable loss of public stature that retirement brings. Chief executives whose retirement dates have been announced often make little jokes about having to get their own coffee or feed quarters into a photocopy machine or take the subway. But these jokes have a bitter edge. Gaylord Freeman, during his last year as chairman of First National Bank of Chicago, said this:

> I came in '34 and go out in '75. . . . Do I feel withdrawal symptoms? . . . Which would you rather be doing: travelling through Europe and calling on the ministers of finance and heads of state, or playing bridge with people who haven't had a new thought in twenty years?

Three years later he added:

> This January, I sat down in the afternoon and read a novel. That's the first one I read since I got out of school in 1934. I never felt I could waste a minute. It [would have been] cheating.

Isn't this amazing? This CEO could not find time in over forty years, even while on vacation, to read a single novel. In my view he cheated his company by *not* reading one. For those who've had no intellectual stimulation outside their work life, those who've pursued no other interests, retirement is a special trauma. But whose fault is that? It's hard to work up a great deal of sympathy for people who suffer from such self-made voids.

The point is that *during* your work life there must be something outside of work, some other compelling interest, some noble cause or absorbing recreation. The chief executive who fails to have this can hardly give full measure to the job. How can one be a whole person if he or she lets the top office be all-controlling, all-consuming? What message does such behavior convey to others?

Hang Around—Or Break Clean?

In any event, here you are. If you've done your job right, you have a solid succession plan. You've shared it with your directors. You've let them know your timetable. And the time for a bow and curtain call is drawing near. What next?

What's next depends on what you've done to prepare yourself for it. First, there is the task of turning over your role to the next player. Let's assume that you've steeled yourself to do just this. A question remains, though, as to whether there's a role left for you. Whether you want it is another question, but more important, should there be such a role?

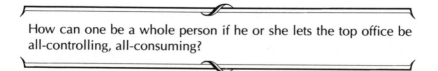

How can one be a whole person if he or she lets the top office be all-controlling, all-consuming?

The answer to these questions depends on your answers to others. Is your successor qualified to hit the ground running? If not, you failed your job at the end, and now it is too late to do much about this. And there are two other questions. What role, if any, does your successor want you to play? And, quite apart from that, what is *your* next role in life?

Some of the most successful CEO transitions occur when the successor is an insider with whom you've had a close and mutually constructive relationship. In this case it may be that there is still some value you can provide to the organization. But remember, that's your successor's call, not yours. And so far as mentoring is concerned, any voluntary advice giving should come to an end the day your successor takes office.

Now as you look back over the years, you may realize that there is much you forgot to pass along and untold amounts of wisdom that you still possess. But you'll discover just how important your wisdom is when you don't receive those telephone calls you'd been expecting, or worse, when offering unsolicited advice you notice a polite glazed look. You'd do better by putting your energies into determining how you can gracefully extricate yourself from your employer and your earlier life as CEO. A clean break is far better than a series of fractures extending over months or years.

What Do You Want to Be When You Grow Up?

It's time, and maybe long past time, for you to reposition yourself. There's a whole new life ahead of you, or at least what remains of one. And what remains of it depends on what you make of it.

Many retired chiefs have gone on to brilliant new careers. Maybe there are other people who could benefit from your wisdom, people who might even appreciate it. You could, like Rene

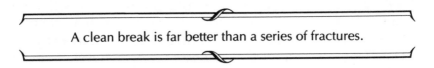

A clean break is far better than a series of fractures.

McPherson of Dana Corporation, become dean of a great school of business. Or, like Arjay Miller of Ford Motor Corporation, help build one. Stanford University benefitted from both. Some CEOs have even become college presidents, but I've yet to find a case in which the college could not have done better. You could head up a great not-for-profit organization, as some have done. You could even become CEO of a corporation on whose board you sit, as did Stanley Gault of Rubbermaid, when he was elected CEO of Goodyear.

But most such post-CEO careers don't develop instantaneously. They require at least some planning and involvement while you're still on active duty. Nevertheless, even if you've foolishly done no planning at all, there are still many exciting options available.

If corporate blood still flows through your veins, you might apply to become an interim chief executive officer at another firm.

Such opportunities are not difficult to explore. Or, if you're interested in another kind of short-term assignment, you might consider spending a few months overseas applying your accumu-
lated know-how to organizations in developing countries or
Eastern Europe or the former Soviet Union.

But if you think you've done your share of international traveling, there are short-term assignments in the United States
where you might help turn around an important nonprofit organization or contribute to the improvement of an educational system. You might hope to get a government post, such as David
Kearns's position as U.S. Deputy Secretary of Education, which
he took upon retirement from Xerox. But for a prestigious and
influential job like this, you'll probably need to display a record
of earlier commitment and on-the-job involvement. Still, there are
other levels of civic or political office you might realistically aspire
to.

Maybe you'd prefer a life of teaching or reflection. You could
write your memoirs. Perhaps members of your family would be
interested in reading them (or perhaps not, depending on how
much they were a part of your life, and you of theirs, when you
were a CEO). If a book seems too ambitious, then how about an
article? Remember, though, that writing history can be risky.

Don Frey, former vice-president, product development at
Ford Motor Company and later CEO of Bell & Howell, celebrated
his life as product champion in an October 1991 *Harvard Business
Review* article. Taking credit for having championed Ford's Mustang (as Iacocca had earlier done, describing himself in his autobiography as its father), Frey explained the art and excitement of
pushing a product to market. A few weeks later, Donald E. Petersen, former Ford CEO, conceded in his new book on management
that Iacocca and Frey had indeed been in the management line-
up but that he and Hal Sperlich were the Mustang's planners. "I
don't think Lee will mind," he wrote, "if I say that Hal Sperlich,
who worked for me, was the key person on the team."

If your ego is still starved for the attention due you for earlier
accomplishments, you could contact a speakers' bureau and hit
the lecture circuit. Don't be too surprised, though, if the promise
of tales of your heroic past fails to please the box office.

Or teaching may be something you've always wanted to take
up. A number of retired CEOs, including Don Frey, are doing this

successfully. But before signing up, consider this report from one who found it more challenging than expected: "My business philosophy and commitment to ethics were brilliantly illustrated by anecdotes that came from my practical experience. But at the end of the first lecture I realized that my war stories wouldn't hold the students' interest for another hour, much less for the whole semester."

You Could Even Retire!

The question is, what do you *want* to do? Maybe you'd even like to retire, *actually* retire.

The possibilities of post-CEO life are limited only by your imagination. For years you've been feeling just a little bit sorry for yourself, hemmed in as you were by responsibilities to others, controlled by an unremitting calendar of twelve-hour days. Now it's *your* turn. And your spouse's. You might want to keep that in mind as well.

It's time to move on, to look forward rather than backward. Whatever legacy you've left is now behind you and rapidly receding. The one thing you *won't* enjoy doing, over the long run, is looking over your successor's shoulder. For one thing, this won't be welcomed. But quite apart from that, you may not like what you see. If an able successor has taken your role, there will be changes made that you would not have made and some that you will not approve of. So to avoid sleepless nights, distance yourself. Find another stage. There are plenty of them around for people of your experience, talent, and capacity.

But perhaps the time has passed for you to strut and fret another hour upon a stage. Maybe you no longer need to march in the corporate parade. How about a good long break? You've paid your dues; you've proved yourself. Maybe it's time to create a future much different from the past.

Will Rogers once said, "We can't all be heroes, because someone has to sit on the curb and clap as they go by." While it's not too helpful to dwell upon the past, a little glimpse backward can't hurt. In taking that glimpse you may decide that you've already been that hero, and now it's time to become something else. Now there's time to sit on that curb and clap, or at least reflect.

Think about what the poet Edna St. Vincent Millay observed: "It is not true that life is one damn thing after another," she wrote. "It's one damn thing over and over."

Looking back, your life as a chief executive was full of two things. Challenge, sometimes excruciating challenge. And rou-

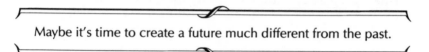

Maybe it's time to create a future much different from the past.

tine. The routine of bureaucracy, for example, the dull frustration of dealing with one regulatory restraint after another. The boredom of certain duties you had to perform, like attending charity dinners. Life was both one damn thing after another and some things over and over.

In looking forward, you now have the freedom to prove the poet wrong. If you're wise, you'll see to it that your life from now on will never be the same thing over and over. The great thing about the future is that it's now a future of your choice. The world is full of stages, and of curbs. Which you choose is now completely up to you.

Good luck!

Notes

Preface

Page

iv   *In visiting Prague less than a year after the "Velvet Revolution," I noted the autobiography of Thomas Bata:* Thomas J. Bata, with Sonja Sinclair, *Bata: Shoemaker to the World* (Don Mills, Ontario: Stoddart, 1990).

xv   *One highly regarded CEO:* John A. Byrne with Dean Foust and Louis Therrien, "Executive Pay," *Business Week* (March 30, 1992), p. 52.

xvi   *In 1990 alone, nearly a million American managers:* Charles F. Hendricks, *The Rightsizing Remedy* (Homewood, IL: Business One Irwin, 1992), p. vii.

Chapter One

MEMORANDUM

Page

1   The memorandum-as-chapter format is not an artifice but stems from the author's experience. In the fall of 1990, the board of trustees of the American Management Association formed a search committee to seek my successor as CEO. After a half-year search, assisted by Heidrick and Struggles, the board selected AMA's president, David Fagiano. In preparation for the transition, I had made copious notes about the role of a CEO, building both on my experience and, more important, on many years of observation and discussions with successful, and unsuccessful, chiefs. When it became clear that Fagiano would be chosen, I

began a series of mentoring sessions based on those notes. On April 1, 1991, the succession date, I conveyed this collection of notes to him with a covering memo similar to this chapter. The rest of the book is a considerable expansion of those notes.

Chapter Two

You've Made It to the Top—Now What?

Page

4   *Donald Perkins:* John A. Byrne and William C. Symonds, "The Best Bosses Avoid the Pitfalls of Power," *Business Week* (April 1, 1991), p. 59.

4   *Tom Watson, Jr.:* From the author's observations while an executive at IBM.

4   *"I think a sense of humility":* Harry Levinson and Stuart Rosenthal, *CEO: Corporate Leadership in Action* (New York: Basic Books, 1984), p. 207.

7   *In 1992, for example, the General Motors Board of Directors:* Steve Lohr, "Pulling Down the Corporate Clubhouse," *The New York Times* (April 12, 1992), Sec 3, p. 1.

8   *As Lee Iacocca advises:* Lee Iacocca with William Novak, *Iacocca: An Autobiography* (New York: Bantam, 1984), p. 161.

9   *Harold Geneen:* Harold Geneen with Alvin Moscow, *Managing* (New York: Doubleday, 1984), p. 37.

9   *In contrast, when Marisa Bellisario:* Thomas R. Horton, *"What Works for Me": 16 CEOs Talk About Their Careers and Commitments* (New York: Random House Business Division, 1986), p. 44.

Chapter Three

Decision Making: Does Rambo Have It Right?

Page

13   *Walter J. Connolly, Jr.:* John A. Byrne, William C. Symonds, and Julia Flynn Siler, "The CEO Disease," *Business Week* (April 1, 1991), p. 55.

Page

15   *When Corning's CEO James Houghton:* Keith M. Hammonds, "Corning's Class Act," *Business Week* (May 13, 1991), p. 70.

15   *As Peter Drucker pointed out:* Peter F. Drucker, *The Effective Executive* (New York: Harper & Row, 1967), p. 143.

16   *In 1983, Gordon Donaldson and Jay Lorsch:* Gordon Donaldson and Jay W. Lorsch, *Decision Making at the Top* (New York: Basic Books, 1983), p. 98.

16   *And despite the many words written about decisions since Chester I. Barnard:* Chester I. Barnard, *The Functions of the Executive*, 30th Anniversary Edition (Cambridge, MA: Harvard University Press, 1966), p. 194.

16   *Robert Crandall:* Robert McGough, "Changing Course," *Financial World* (July 23, 1991), p. 44.

17   *Retailing giant Ralph Lazarus:* Robert L. Shook, *The Chief Executive Officers* (New York: Harper & Row, 1981), p. 109.

18   *In the early 1980s, Harry Levinson and Stuart Rosenthal:* Levinson and Rosenthal, *CEO*, p. 282.

18   *Reverend John Cavanaugh:* Horton, "What Works for Me," p. 399.

Chapter Four

Climbing the Learning Curve

Page

21   *In an interview with Harvard Business School professor John J. Gabarro:* John J. Gabarro, *The Dynamics of Taking Charge* (Cambridge, MA: Harvard Business School Press, 1987), p. 1.

21   *Peter G. Scotese:* Horton, "What Works for Me," p. 130.

22   *According to Charles Lazarus:* Richard C. Whiteley, *The Customer-Driven Company* (Reading, MA: Addison-Wesley, 1991), p. 39.

22   *Donald Coggiola:* Carol J. Loomis, "Can John Akers Save IBM?" *Fortune* (July 15, 1991), p. 56.

22   *Thomas Alva Edison:* "Time Travel," *Life* (Summer Special 1991), vol. 14, no. 6, p. 46.

23   *Some years ago, Xerox:* Brian Dumaine, "The Bureaucracy Busters," *Fortune* (June 17, 1991), p. 42.

Page

24   *Jacques Maisonrouge:* Thomas R. Horton, "Memo for Manage-
        ment," *Management Review* (July 1983), p. 3.

24   *Instead, you need to become what Charlotte L. Beers:* Horton, "What
        Works for Me," p. 217.

24   *A study by Harvard professor John J. Gabarro:* Gabarro, *The Dynamics
        of Taking Charge,* pp. 84–85.

25   *A second reason for failure:* Ibid., p. 8.

26   *When Toshihiko Yamashita:* Toshihiko Yamashita, *The Panasonic Way:
        From a Chief Executive's Desk* (Tokyo and New York: Kodansha,
        1987), p. 26.

26   *"We were in trouble":* Ibid., p. 24.

26   *The lifeblood of Matsushita's divisional organization:* Ibid., p. 34.

27   *When Lee Iacocca became CEO:* Iacocca with Novak, *Iacocca,* pp.
        161–162.

27   *Iacocca recalls:* Ibid., p. 175.

27   *Yamashita remembers his first days:* Yamashita, *The Panasonic Way,*
        p. 26.

27   *The founder of the company, Konosuke Matsushita:* Ibid., p. 38.

27   *For example, on his first day as chairman of Alcoa:* Author's personal
        conversation with Paul O'Neill, April 7, 1990; see also Thomas
        A. Stewart, "A New Way to Wake Up a Giant," *Fortune* (October
        22, 1990), p. 91.

Chapter Five

Planning: The Job You Can't Delegate

Page

29   *Before beginning any planning session:* Harold Geneen, *Managing*
        (Garden City, NY: Doubleday, 1984), p. 98.

30   *Defined by Hugh McDonald:* Thomas A. Stewart, "Brain Power,"
        Fortune (June 3, 1991), p. 44.

31   *According to Sören Olsson:* Sören Olsson, "Strategic Change at
        Apple Computer" (Presentation made at Management Centre
        Europe's Top Management Forum, Paris, June 25, 1991).

31   *In 1963, shortly after Arthur ("Punch") Ochs Sulzberger:* Levinson
        and Rosenthal, *CEO,* p. 225.

Page

31   *Some years ago, while on a trip to California:* Tom Ashton, "N.B.,"
      Chief Executive (June 1991), p. 18.

32   *Peter Drucker describes what he calls systematic abandonment:* Peter F.
      Drucker, *Managing in Turbulent Times* (New York: Harper & Row,
      1980), p. 43.

32   *In his classic book:* Peter F. Drucker, *The Practice of Management*
      (New York: Harper Brothers, 1954), pp. 29–33.

32   *In 1918, Henry Ford:* Robert Lacey, *Ford: The Men and the Machine*
      (Boston: Little, Brown, 1986), p. 104.

32   *With characteristic prescience, Drucker ended his account:* Drucker,
      The Practice of Management, p. 33.

32   *Meanwhile, in the small town of Bentonville:* Bill Saporito, "Is Wal-
      Mart Unstoppable?" *Fortune* (May 6, 1991), p. 51.

33   *The* kaizen *concept:* Masaaki Imai, *Kaizen: The Key to Japan's Com-
      petitive Success* (New York: Random House Business Division,
      1986), p. xxix.

33   *According to Richard A. Zimmerman:* Thomas R. Horton, *"What
      Works for Me,"* p. 237.

33   *For example, Hershey:* Author's conversation with Hershey's CEO
      Richard A. Zimmerman, April 6, 1991.

34   *A dramatic example of the power of such ideas:* Laurie Kretchman,
      "On the Rise," *Fortune* (July 15, 1991), p. 122.

34   *Microsoft chairman William H. Gates 3rd:* "MicroSoft's Rise," *The
      1991 Business Week 1000* (July 23, 1991), pp. 20–21.

34   *H. Wayne Huizenga:* Richard Sandomir, "Wayne Huizenga's
      Growth Complex," *The New York Times Magazine, Part II* (June
      1991), p. 2.

35   *Sandra L. Kurtzig:* Sandra L. Kurtzig with Tom Parker, *CEO:
      Building a $400 Million Company from the Ground Up* (New York:
      W. W. Norton, 1991), p. 43.

35   *Realizing that ASK couldn't be all things to all companies:* Ibid., pp.
      130–131.

35   *In the 1940s, Chester Barnard:* Chester I. Barnard, *Organization and
      Management* (Cambridge, MA: Harvard University Press, 1948),
      p. 80.

Chapter Six

Those Lonesome CEO Blues

Page

36   *Abraham Lincoln:* Louis W. Koenig, *The Chief Executive* (New York: Harcourt, Brace & World, 1964), p. 349.

36   *As Truman said:* Merle Miller, *Plain Speaking: An Oral Biography of Harry S Truman* (New York: Berkley, 1973), p. 200.

37   *A survey by Catalyst:* Susan B. Garland, "How to Keep Women Managers on the Corporate Ladder," *Business Week* (September 2, 1991), p. B4.

37   *"Assume," says University of Georgia professor Dawn D. Bennett-Alexander:* Walter Kiechel 3rd, "A Guide for the Expectant Executive," *Fortune* (September 9, 1991), p. 191.

37   *William Rainey Harper:* Clark Kerr and Marian L. Gade, *The Many Lives of Academic Presidents* (Washington, DC: Association of Governing Boards of Universities and Colleges, 1986), p. 224.

38   *Father John Cavanaugh:* Ibid., p. 207.

38   *Harold W. Dodds:* Ibid., p. 201.

38   *Former Yale University president:* Ibid., p. 32.

39   *Though AT&T Chairman Robert E. Allen:* Peter Coy, "Robert Allen," *The 1991 Business Week 1000*, p. 89.

39   *Benjamin Ide Wheeler:* Kerr and Gade, *Academic Presidents*, p. 92.

39   *Henry W. Wriston:* Ibid., p. 194.

41   *As president of The Conference Board, Kenneth Randall:* Isadore Barmash, *The Chief Executives* (Philadelphia: J. B. Lippincott, 1978), p. 223.

41   *Perhaps Kenneth Patchen's "Lonesome Boy Blues":* Bartlett's, p. 879.

Chapter Seven

Delegation and Team Building: No Solo Acts, Please

Page

42   *Jeffrey Sonnenfeld:* Doran P. Levin, "Detroit Abuzz: Who After Iacocca?" *The New York Times* (July 15, 1991), p. C1.

43   *Lee Iacocca:* Ibid.

Page

43   *In contrast, PepsiCo's Wayne D. Calloway:* "A Different Brand of Leader," *Chief Executive* (July/August 1991), p. 41.

43   *A recent internal study by PepsiCo:* Brian Moskal, "Arrogance: The Executive Achilles' Heel," *Industry Week* (June 3, 1991), p. 19.

44   *Don G. Mitchell:* Don G. Mitchell, *Top Man: Reflections of a Chief Executive* (New York: AMACOM, 1970), p. 49.

45   *Father Theodore M. Hesburgh:* Horton, "What Works for Me," p. 161.

46   *Yet when he landed at American Express:* John P. Kotter, *A Force for Change: How Leadership Differs From Management* (New York: The Free Press, 1990), p. 40.

47   *Don Mitchell describes the two basic reasons:* Mitchell, *Top Man,* p. 41.

47   *As Henry Kissinger says:* Henry A. Kissinger, *The Executive Dialogue Series* (General Electric, May 23, 1991), p. 2.

47   *Arthur K. Watson:* Author's personal conversation with Mr. Watson in 1966.

48   *Entrepreneur Portia Isaacson:* Horton, "What Works for Me," pp. 316–317.

48   *When Yves Trellu was president and chief operating officer:* Author's interview with Mr. Trellu, October 30, 1985.

50   *Portia Isaacson says:* Horton, "What Works for Me," p. 322.

50   *Harvard Business School professor John J. Gabarro's research:* Gabarro, *The Dynamics of Taking Charge,* p. 8.

50   *Although Robert Crandall, CEO of American Airlines:* McGough, "Changing Course," p. 43.

51   *Disney CEO Michael Eisner:* Ron Grover, *The Disney Touch* (Homewood, IL: Business One Irwin), 1991, p. 61.

51   *In 1989, Elliott Jaques:* Elliott Jaques, *Requisite Organization* (Arlington, VA: Cason Hall, 1989), pp. 16–19.

52   *Nordstrom, Inc.:* Francine Schwadell, "Nordstrom Taps 4 Non-Family Members for Newly Created Post of Co-President," *The Wall Street Journal* (May 21, 1991), p. C9.

52   *In 1992, for example, Microsoft:* Harris Collingwood, "In Business This Week," *Business Week* (February 17, 1992), p. 46.

52   *. . . and Xerox, a six-member "corporate office":* Suein L. Hwang, "Xerox Forms New Structure for Printer, Copier Business, Cre-

Page

ates New Office," *The Wall Street Journal* (February 5, 1992), p. B6.

53   *The impulsiveness of IBM's Chairman Thomas J. Watson, Jr.:* Author's personal observation while employed by IBM, 1954–1982.

52   *In his autobiography, Watson wrote:* Thomas J. Watson, Jr., and Peter Petre, *Father Son & Co.* (New York: Bantam, 1990), p. 249.

53   *Honda Motor Company, Ltd.:* Tetsuo Sakiya, *Honda Motor: The Men, The Management, The Machines* (Tokyo and New York: Kodansha, 1982), p. 65.

53   *When Walt Disney Co. needed new leadership:* John Huey, "Secrets of Great Second Bananas," *Fortune* (May 6, 1991), p. 64.

53   *At Coca-Cola Co.:* Ibid.

53   *At Capitol Cities/ABC, Inc.:* Ibid.

53   *In 1991, Fox, Inc., chairman Barry Diller:* Kathryn Harris, "Madame Chairman," *Forbes* (August 5, 1991), p. 108.

53   *(However, only a half-year later:* Richard W. Stevenson, "Head of Fox Studio Resigns to Pursue His Own Ventures," *The New York Times* (February 25, 1992), p. A1.

53   *C. Fred Fetterolf:* Dana Milbank, "Alcoa's President Fetterolf Leaves Firm Over Differences With Chairman O'Neill," *The Wall Street Journal* (July 31, 1991), p. B4.

53   *In early 1992, for example, Time Warner's co-chief executive:* Roger Cohen, "A Divorce in the Executive Suite," *The New York Times* (February 24, 1992), p. C1.

54   *In July 1991, The New York Times:* Michael Lev, "President of Kemper to Add Chairman's Post," *The New York Times* (July 17, 1991), p. C4.

54   *About a week later the* Times *reported:* Anthony Ramirez, "A President Is Chosen at American Express," *The New York Times* (July 23, 1991), p. C4.

54   *Only a few months later, Golub added two more titles:* Kurt Eichenwald, "A Top Official Resigns at American Express," *The New York Times* (October 29, 1991), p. D5.

54   *Business writer Anthony J. Michels:* Anthony J. Michels, "Chief Executives As Idi Amin?" *Fortune* (July 1, 1991), p. 13.

54   *Donald C. Hambrick:* Ibid.

54   *But Brunswick Corporation's chairman, president, and CEO Jack S. Reichert:* Ibid.

Page

55   *Robert W. Lear:* Robert W. Lear, "The Three Stages of a CEO," *Chief Executive* (July/August 1991), p. 14.

55   *Research by Professor Donald C. Hambrick:* Donald C. Hambrick, Presentation at Management Centre Europe's 1991 Top Management Forum, Paris, June 24, 1991.

Chapter Eight

Making Time: The Impossible Dream?

Page

58   *About forty years ago, a study was made in Sweden:* Drucker, *The Practice of Management*, p. 165.

58   *Some years later, Henry Mintzberg:* Henry Mintzberg, "The Manager's Job: Folklore and Fact," in Harry Levinson, ed., *Designing and Managing Your Career* (Cambridge, MA: Harvard Business School Press, 1989), pp. 47–57.

58   *Professor Leonard R. Sayles:* Ibid., p. 57.

59   *According to the University of Maryland's John P. Robinson:* Carol Hymowitz, "Trading Fat Paychecks for Free Time," *The Wall Street Journal* (August 5, 1991), p. B1.

59   *One woman puts it this way:* Mark Baker, *Women: American Women in Their Own Words* (New York: Pocket Star Books, 1991), p. 227.

60   *One person who has studied these questions for over twenty years:* Alec MacKenzie, *The Time Trap* (New York: AMACOM, 1990), p. vii.

63   *Take time especially to develop a good working relationship with your assistant:* Horton, "What Works for Me," p. 119.

64   *Jack Welch:* William Safire and Leonard Safir, *Leadership* (New York: Simon and Schuster, 1990), p. 243.

Chapter Nine

Ambition and Greed, or How to Lose by Winning

Page

66   *Ted Turner:* Studs Terkel, *American Dreams: Lost and Found* (New York: Pantheon, 1980), pp. 66–69.

Page

67   *Wallace Rasmussen:* Ibid., pp. 14–16.

67   *Former Salomon Brothers chairman John Gutfreund:* Andrew Murr and Joshua Hammer with Joanna Stone, "One Bluff Too Many," *Newsweek* (August 26, 1991), p. 32.

67   *A few years earlier, in 1988, former boy wonder:* Bryan Burrough and John Helyar, *Barbarians at the Gate: The Fall of RJR Nabisco* (New York: Harper Perennial, 1991), p. 28.

68   *In 1991, the nation watched as Clark Clifford:* C-SPAN television coverage, September 1991.

68   *In a speech to a group of lawyers:* Stephen Labaton, "Directors of First American Are Admonished on B.C.C.I.," *The New York Times* (September 28, 1991), p. 17.

68   *According to* Business Week: John A. Byrne, "The Flap Over Executive Pay," *Business Week* (May 6, 1991), p. 90.

68   *And, as this book went to press:* Jerry Schwartz, "Coke's Chairman Defends $86 Million Pay and Bonus," *The New York Times* (April 16, 1992), p. C1.

69   *And now, even as many observers:* Stephanie Losee, "Posthumous Paychecks for Chief Executives," *Fortune* (October 7, 1991), p. 13.

69   *But A. F. Kaulakis:* A. F. Kaulakis, Letter to the Editor, *Business Week* (May 27, 1991), p. 7.

69   *In 1990, Lee Iacocca:* John A. Byrne, "Pay Stubs of the Rich and Corporate," *Business Week* (May 7, 1990), p. 56.

70   *Perhaps to mollify him:* Doron P. Levin, "Iacocca Compensation: $4.58 Million Last Year," *The New York Times* (April 13, 1991), p. 19.

70   *In 1985, Allegheny International's CEO Robert J. Buckley:* William C. Symonds, "Big Trouble at Allegheny," *Business Week* (August 11, 1986), p. 56.

70   *Even after this sale:* Brett Duval Fromson, "The Slow Death of E. F. Hutton," *Fortune* (February 29, 1988), p. 82.

71   *Its CEO, Robert Fomon:* Ibid.

71   *Amy Saltzman:* Amy Saltzman, *Down-Shifting: Reinventing Success on a Slower Track* (New York: Harper Collins, 1991), pp. 26–28.

71   *Richard Pinto:* Ibid., p. 26.

71   *Edith Gilson:* Ibid., p. 27.

73   *In March 1991, Rick Chollet:* David Gelman with Carolyn Friday, "Overstressed by Success," *Newsweek* (June 3, 1991), p. 56.

Page

73   *Washington psychoanalyst Douglas LaDier:* Ibid.

73   *Psychotherapist Steven Berglas:* Ibid.

73   *Richard O. Jacobs:* Richard O. Jacobs, *Crash Landing: Surviving a Business Crisis* (Macomb, IL: Glenbridge, 1991), pp. 4, 33.

74   *It's a symptom of what's been called the "CEO disease":* Byrne, Symonds, and Siler, "CEO Disease," p. 52.

Chapter Ten
Coping and Growing: A Self-Renewal Process

Page

75   *Corporate psychiatric consultant Gerald Kraines:* Gelman with Friday, "Overstressed," p. 56.

76   *A long-retired friend:* Author's conversation with George Perkins of White Plains, New York, 1970.

76   *Robert A. Beck:* Shook, *The Chief Executive Officers,* p. 22.

77   *Irving S. Shapiro:* Ibid., p. 217.

77   *Kenneth R. Dubuque:* L. A. Winokur, "Vacations Are Becoming Part of the Job," *The Wall Street Journal* (July 16, 1991), p. B1.

77   *To get away from your job* and *the fax:* Nancy Marx Better, "Roughing It on Dude Ranches Helps Executives to Unwind," *The Daytona Beach Sunday News Journal* (July 21, 1991), p. E1.

77   *Dallas's Timberlawn Psychiatric Hospital:* Gelman with Friday, "Overstressed," p. 56.

78   *If you wish to dig still deeper:* Nancy Marx Better, "Tied in Knots? Unravel With a Trip to Childhood," *The New York Times* (July 21, 1991), p. F21.

78   *Indeed, studies have shown that the most stressful jobs:* Allan L. Otten, "People Patterns: Firefighters, Waiters Have Stress in Common," *The Wall Street Journal* (July 26, 1991), p. B1.

79   *In* The Seasons of a Man's Life: Daniel J. Levinson, *The Seasons of a Man's Life* (New York: Ballantine, 1978), p. 91.

Chapter Eleven
Going Global: How to Become a World-Class Manager

Page

82   *Professor Robert Reich:* Robert Reich, "The Myth of 'Made in the U.S.A.,' " *The Wall Street Journal* (July 5, 1991), p. A6.

Page

82   *Honeywell chairman and CEO James J. Renier:* Louis Therrien, "Honeywell Is Finally Tasting the Sweet Life," *Business Week* (June 3, 1991), p. 34.

82   *The recent U.S. export boom:* Peter F. Drucker, "Secrets of the U.S. Export Boom," *The Wall Street Journal* (August 1, 1991), p. A12.

83   *Leslie M. Schweitzer:* Letter to the author, September 26, 1991.

85   *Though English has become the international language of business, economist Paul McCracken observes:* Paul McCracken, Presentation at American Management Association's Finance Conference, May 1985.

86   *Eugenia Ulasewitz:* Stephanie Strom, "Retailing's Modest Napoleon," *The New York Times* (September 29, 1991), p. F12.

87   *A recent survey by Dunhill Personnel Systems:* Stuart Feldman, "Losing the Home Field Advantage," *Management Review* (September 1991), p. 7.

88   *Anthony J. F. O'Reilly:* Anthony J. F. O'Reilly, "The Emergence of the Global Consumer," *Directors & Boards* (Winter 1991), p. 12.

89   *One associate says:* Thomas F. O'Boyle, "Inspired by His Roots, Heinz's Tony O'Reilly Demands More, Better," *The Wall Street Journal* (April 1, 1992), p. 1.

89   *Ken Iverson:* Richard Preston, *American Steel* (Englewood Cliffs, NJ: Prentice-Hall, 1991).

89   *James R. Houghton:* Hammonds, "Corning's Class Act," p. 68.

89   *Stanley Gault:* Erik Calonius, "Smart Moves by Quality Champs," *Fortune 1991/The New American Century* (special edition), 1991, p. 28.

89   *When Gault retired:* Zachary Schiller, "Goodyear May Be Getting Some Traction at Last," *Business Week* (October 7, 1991), p. 38.

Chapter Twelve

Manage by the Bottom Line — Or to It?

Page

91   *Indeed, Peter Drucker has described profitability:* Drucker, *The Practice of Management*, p. 35.

92   *At ITT one major innovation, as he called it:* Geneen with Moscow, p. 86.

Page

95   *In 1991, ninety-three U.S. companies:* Alan Deutschman, "America's Fastest Risers," *Fortune* (October 7, 1991), p. 46.

96   *Drucker points out:* Drucker, *The Practice of Management,* p. 37.

97   *Business writer John Thackrey:* Thomas R. Horton and Peter C. Reid, *Beyond the Trust Gap: Forging a New Partnership Between Managers and Their Employees* (Homewood, IL: Business One Irwin, 1991), p. 56.

98   *One of the most intense is reported to be Laurence A. Tisch:* Ken Auletta, *Three Blind Mice: How the TV Networks Lost Their Way* (New York: Random House, 1991), p. 583.

98   *Though the CBS Board named him as acting chief executive:* Ibid., p. 182.

Chapter Thirteen

Corporate Culture: Ignore It at Your Peril

Page

101   *Indeed, Professor Edgar H. Schein:* Edgar H. Schein, *Organizational Culture and Leadership* (San Francisco: Jossey-Bass Publishers, 1985), p. 2.

102   *Southwest Airlines:* Peter C. T. Elsworth, "Southwest Air's New Push West," *The New York Times* (June 16, 1991), p. F5.

102   *SWA's senior executives spend one day each quarter:* Letter from management development consultant Frances E. Willis to author, October 2, 1991.

102   *According to one airline analyst:* Elsworth, "Southwest Air's New Push West," p. F5.

102   *The General Electric Company:* Levinson and Rosenthal, *CEO,* pp. 18–25.

103   *Welch then went to work on the challenging job:* John P. Kotter, *A Force For Change: How Leadership Differs From Management* (New York: The Free Press, 1990), p. 51.

103   *To do so he used a variety of methodologies:* Thomas A. Stuart, "GE Keeps Those Ideas Coming," *Fortune* (August 12, 1991), pp. 42–43.

104   *Though the business press gives GE credit:* Ibid., p. 41.

104   *For as Rodger Bricknell:* Ibid., p. 49.

Page

105   *By 1992, Welch began to shed:* John Holusha, "A Call for Kinder
        Managers at G.E.," *The New York Times* (March 4, 1992), p. D1.

105   *In 1991, then age 73 and fighting an incurable bone cancer, Walton:*
        John Huey, "America's Most Successful Merchant," *Fortune*
        (September 23, 1991), p. 48.

106   *The fabled Stew Leonard's Dairy Store:* Author's observation.

106   *Some years ago, a culture was defined:* Terrence E. Deal and Allan
        A. Kennedy, *Corporate Cultures: The Rites and Rituals of Corporate
        Life* (Reading, MA: Addison-Wesley, 1982), p. 15.

106   *According to Tom Watson, Jr.:* Thomas J. Watson, Jr., *A Business and
        Its Beliefs: The Ideas That Helped Build IBM* (New York: McGraw-
        Hill, 1963), p. 15.

106   *Twenty-five years earlier, one example:* Author's private conversa-
        tion in 1957 with the former prisoner, then a manager in IBM's
        U.S. operation.

107   *"We are trying to become a $60-billion global company":* Martha H.
        Peak, "Anti-Manager Named Manager of the Year," *Management
        Review* (October 1991), p. 7.

107   *Or, as Stanford Business School professor Richard Pascale says:* Pre-
        sentation by Richard Pascale at Management Centre Europe's
        Top Management Forum, Paris, June 25, 1991.

107   *For example, after British Airways was privatized:* Leonard D. Good-
        stein and W. Warner Burke, "Creating Successful Organization
        Change," *Organizational Dynamics* (Spring 1991), pp. 9–12.

108   *Whirlpool Corporation:* Presentation by Jan Prising at Management
        Centre Europe's Top Management Forum, Paris, June 25, 1991.

109   *Peter Drucker reminds us:* Peter F. Drucker, "Don't Change Cor-
        porate Culture—Use It!" *The Wall Street Journal* (March 28, 1991),
        p. 13.

110   *According to Max DePree:* Max DePree, *Leadership Is an Art* (Gar-
        den City, NY: Doubleday, 1989), p. 9.

Chapter Fourteen

Management Style: You've Gotta Be You

Page

111   *Michael Maccoby:* Michael Maccoby, *The Leader: A New Face for
        American Management* (New York: Simon and Schuster, 1981),
        p. 17.

Page

111   *James MacGregor Burns:* James MacGregor Burns, *Leadership* (New York: Harper Torchbooks, 1978), p. 4.

112   *Irving Shapiro:* David Diamond, "Who's the Boss?" *The Wall Street Journal Book of Chief Executive Style* (New York: William Morrow, 1989), p. 13.

112   *In 1991, when Debora de Hoyos:* Barbara Presley Nobel, "Ms. Managing Partner," *The New York Times* (August 11, 1991), p. 12.

112   *In 1988, Bernard B. Beal:* Diana B. Henriques, "Piercing Wall Street's 'Lucite Ceiling,' " *The New York Times* (August 11, 1991), Sec. III, p. 1.

114   *Robert Fierle:* Author's conversation with Mr. Fierle, March 1990.

114   *One former Pan Am executive described Trippe:* "Pan Am: The Fall of a Legend," *Conde Nast Traveler* (July 1991), p. 23.

114   *In contrast, Herbert Kelleher:* Peter C. T. Elsworth, "Not Just Another Elvis Impersonator," *The New York Times* (June 16, 1991), p. F5.

115   *For example, in the mid-1980s, Hicks Waldron:* Sonny Kleinfield, *Staying at the Top: The Life of a CEO* (New York: New American Library, 1986), p. 263.

115   *And a few CEOs, such as . . . William Farley:* Timothy D. Schellhardt, "Farley to Cede Pepperell Unit's Majority Stake," *The Wall Street Journal* (August 6, 1991), p. A3.

116   *Many years ago . . . John W. Gardner:* John W. Gardner, "Personal Renewal," *The McKinsey Quarterly* (1991), no. 2, p. 81.

Chapter Fifteen

A Touch of Class: How Others See You and What You Can Do About It

Page

119   *Jan Yager:* Jan Yager, *Business Protocol: How to Survive and Succeed in Business* (New York: Wiley, 1991), p. 4.

119   *In a large-scale project commissioned by the American Management Association:* Richard E. Boyatzis, *The Competent Manager* (New York: Wiley, 1982), p. 85.

120   *But John Diebold:* Author's observation.

Page

120   *According to business writer James P. Sterba:* James P. Sterba,
        "Clothes: Packaging the CEO," *The Wall Street Journal Book of
        Chief Executive Style* (New York: Morrow, 1989), pp. 64–66.

121   *When Cathleen Black was publisher of* USA Today: Kathy Crimmins,
        "The Adventures of Emily Post-Feminists," *WSJ Book of Chief Exe-
        cutive Style,* p. 266.

122   *Frank Pace:* Author's observation.

122   *In sharp contrast, Admiral Hyman Rickover:* Author's observation
        during visits to his office as a computer vendor, 1956–1957.

123   *Letitia Baldrige:* Letitia Baldrige, *Letitia Baldrige's Complete Guide To
        Executive Manners,* edited by Sandi Gelles-Cole (New York: Raw-
        son Associates, 1985), p. 14.

Chapter Sixteen

The Energizing Power of Passion

Page

126   *Ken Iverson:* Richard Preston, *American Steel* (New York: Prentice
        Hall, 1991), p. 8.

127   *Anthony O'Reilly:* "Heinz Meanz Brands," *Chief Executive* (July/
        August, 1990), p. 43.

127   *Joichi Aoi:* Richard Myer, "We Just Stay With It," *Financial World*
        (October 15, 1991), p. 50.

127   *Instead, when asked about his company's core competency:* "Heinz
        Meanz Brands," p. 44.

130   *Some strong chief executives with long tenures, like Armand Hammer:*
        Patricia O'Toole, "The House That Hammer Built," *Lear's* (Octo-
        ber 1991), p. 21.

131   *Max DePree:* Max DePree, *Leadership Is an Art* (New York: Dell,
        1989), p. 135.

Chapter Seventeen

Passing the Torch—But to Whom?

Page

134   *Juan T. Trippe:* Jeffrey Sonnenfeld, *The Hero's Farewell: What Hap-
        pens When CEOs Retire* (New York: Oxford University Press,
        1988), p. 104.

Page

134   *Meanwhile, Trippe continued to roam:* "Pan Am: The Fall of a Legend," p. 21.

134   *In 1939, Trippe's board of directors:* Sonnenfeld, *The Hero's Farewell*, p. 102.

134   *Armand Hammer:* O'Toole, "The House That Hammer Built," p. 21.

136   *In 1953, Ralph J. Cordiner:* Drucker, *The Practice of Management*, p. 170.

136   *In 1981, James D. Robinson 3rd:* Shook, *The Chief Executive Officers*, p. 201.

137   *Two years later, Harvey Golub:* David B. Hilder, "American Express Co. Promotes Golub, Posts 20% Drop in 2nd-Quarter Profit," *The Wall Street Journal* (July 23, 1991), p. B4.

137   *Barely three months later, Golub took on an additional assignment:* Kurt Eichenwald, "A Top Official Resigns at American Express," *The New York Times* (October 29, 1991), p. C4.

137   *As Lee Iacocca approached age 65:* Alex Taylor 3rd, "Lee Iacocca's Prolonged Sayonara," *Fortune* (October 7, 1991), p. 12.

137   *By early 1992, the intrigue at Chrysler:* Bradley A. Stertz, "Driving Back: Chrysler Is Making Solid Progress in Spite of Executive Turmoil," *The Wall Street Journal* (March 3, 1992), p. A1.

138   *Meanwhile, at IBM:* "IBM Officer Will Retire; Pay Cuts Due," *The New York Times* (February 25, 1992), p. C1.

138   *In March 1992, Chrysler's directors:* "Eaton of GM for Top Posts," *The Wall Street Journal* (March 16, 1992), p. A3.

138   *In early 1991, Richard P. Banis:* Michael Lev, "President of Casino Quits Over Succession," *The New York Times* (July 24, 1991), p. D5.

138   *Harry Gray:* Sonnenfeld, *The Hero's Farewell*, pp. 108ff.

139   *In 1990, the Allied-Signal board:* Barnaby J. Fader, "Allied Picks Chief and Wall St. Approves," *The New York Times* (June 28, 1991), p. C1.

140   *In recent years, outsiders have represented more than one-fourth:* Bruce Hager with Lisa Driscoll, Joseph Weber, and Gary McWilliams, "CEO Wanted. No Insiders, Please," *Business Week* (August 12, 1991), p. 44.

140   *Laura Ashley's from Thorn EMI:* Francine Schwadel, "Laura Ashley Chooses New Chief From Beyond World of Fashion," *The Wall Street Journal* (July 18, 1991), p. B1.

Page

140   *This is confirmed by a recent study by A. T. Kearney:* Karen Padley,
        "Where to Look for People Who Can Get Things Done," *Inves-
        tor's Daily* (June 20, 1991), p. 1.

140   *For example, Robert R. Ferguson 3rd:* Agis Salpukas, "New Conti-
        nental Chief Keeps Out of Spotlight," *The New York Times* (Au-
        gust 23, 1991), p. C3.

140   *John A. Thompson:* John A. Thompson, "Interim Executives: The
        Boom in Short-Timers," *The Corporate Board* (September/October
        1991), p. 19.

Chapter Eighteen

Moving On: Is There Life After Retirement?

Page

143   *Former Harvard professor Jeffrey Sonnenfeld:* Sonnenfeld, *The Hero's
        Farewell*, p. 7.

144   *In 1984, as the directors of United Technologies:* Thomas J. Lueck,
        "Gray Still Dogged By Same Charges," *The New York Times* (No-
        vember 30, 1984), p. D1.

144   *Charles Bluhdorn:* Sonnenfeld, *The Hero's Farewell*, p. 106.

144   *Such as an English professor at Clarion University:* Scott Heller, "Vet-
        eran Faculty Member Writes Frankly About Working at an 'Invis-
        ible College,' " *The Chronicle of Higher Education* (October 2,
        1991), p. A17.

145   *Gaylord Freeman:* Terkel, *American Dreams*, p. 18.

148   *Don Frey:* Don Frey, "Learning the Ropes: My Life As a Product
        Champion," *Harvard Business Review* (September/October 1991),
        p. 46.

148   *A few weeks later, Donald E. Petersen:* James B. Treece, "How Ford
        Did It," *Business Week* (October 14, 1991), p. 26.

Index